Classic Classroom Activities

THE OXFORD
Picture
Dictionary
PROGRAM

RENÉE WEISS • JAYME ADELSON-GOLDSTEIN • NORMA SHAPIRO

OXFORD

Oxford University Press
198 Madison Avenue
New York, NY 10016 USA

Great Clarendon Street
Oxford OX2 6DP England

Oxford New York
Athens Auckland Bangkok Bogotá Buenos Aires
Calcutta Cape Town Chennai Dar es Salaam
Delhi Florence Hong Kong Istanbul Karachi
Kuala Lumpur Madrid Melbourne Mexico City
Mumbai Nairobi Paris São Paulo Singapore
Taipei Tokyo Toronto Warsaw

And associated companies in
Berlin Ibadan

www.picturedictionary.org

OXFORD is a trademark of Oxford University Press.

ISBN 0-19-435186-6

Copyright © 1999 Oxford University Press

Library of Congress Cataloging-in-Publication Data

Weiss, Renée.
    Classic classroom activities for the Oxford picture
dictionary / Renée Weiss, Jayme Adelson-Goldstein,
Norma Shapiro.
        p.   cm.
    ISBN 0-19-435186-6
    1. English language—Textbooks for foreign speakers.
    2. English language—Problems, exercises, etc.
    3. Shapiro, Norma. Oxford picture dictionary.
I. Adelson-Goldstein, Jayme. II. Shapiro, Norma.
III. Weiss, Renée. Oxford picture dictionary. IV. Title.
PE1128.W4267   1999   99-13455
428.2'4—dc21

Editorial Manager: Susan Lanzano
Editor: Lynne Barsky
Senior Production Editor: Robyn F. Clemente
Design Project Manager: Lynne Torrey
Senior Art Buyer: Alexandra F. Rockafellar
Art Buyer: Donna Goldberg
Production Manager: Abram Hall
Production Coordinator: Shanta Persaud

Printing (last digit): 10 9 8 7 6 5 4 3 2

ʾnted in the United States.

Illustrations by Annie Bissett, David Cain, Tom Newsom,
Karen Pietrobono, Zina Saunders, Tom Sperling/Craven
Design, Gary Undercuffler, Anna Veltfort, Nina Wallace,
Patrick J. Welsh

Cover design by Lynne Torrey

Authors' Acknowledgments
The authors would like to offer our sincere thanks to the
Oxford University Press publishing team for their hard work
on *Classic Classroom Activities* for *The Oxford Picture
Dictionary*, and acknowledge our colleagues and fellow
authors in *The Oxford Picture Dictionary* program: Marjorie
Fuchs, Margaret Bonner, Lori Howard, Elizabeth Hanson-
Smith, and Evelyn Fella.

We would especially like to thank the following people who
contributed their unique talents and skills to this book:

Susan Lanzano, Editorial Manager, whose expertise and
sensitivity supported this project from conception to birth;

Lynne Barsky and Shirley Brod, Editors, whose keen minds
vigorously analyzed each activity and whose sympathetic ears
took us through each revision of manuscript and art;

Robyn Flusser Clemente, Senior Production Editor, whose
meticulous scrutiny of each page kept us honest; and,

Lynne Torrey, Design Project Manager, who imagined the
book as it might be.

In addition, Renee would like to thank Rheta Goldman,
Sandra Brown, Frank Marsala, and Anne Stumpo-Sanchez of
Los Angeles Unified School District, for their guidance,
teaching support, and friendship.

*This book is lovingly dedicated to my incredible husband,
Malcolm Loeb, and my precious daughter, Sophie Rose, both
of whom are the words and the music in my life. And to my
dear friend Paul, thanks for starting me on the path. -RW*

*To Joanne Abing, whose skills and sense of humor enlighten
and delight. -JAG*

*To Anna and Isidor Baruch, whose journey to Ellis Island
continues to inspire me. -NS*

Table of Contents

12. Recreation

Introduction

Welcome to *Classic Classroom Activities*, a teacher resource book containing over 130 reproducible activities which foster meaningful student-to-student interaction and develop cooperative critical thinking and problem-solving skills. The activities, suitable for beginning through intermediate-level adult and young adult ESL students, incorporate the topics and vocabulary from *The Oxford Picture Dictionary*. Each activity strengthens students' accuracy and fluency in listening to and speaking English as well as provides opportunities for reading and writing skills at the word and sentence level.

We hope this resource helps you and your students reach your classroom goals with a boost of energy and enjoyment!

1. WHAT ARE THE PRINCIPLES BEHIND *CLASSIC CLASSROOM ACTIVITIES*?

The content and methodology found in *Classic Classroom Activities* combine both "classic" and innovative approaches and principles in ESL teaching:

- **Students benefit from communicative activities in varied group configurations.**
  Classic Classroom Activities contains activities where students work individually, in pairs, in small groups, and with the whole class. In addition, many of the activities require students to switch from one grouping to another in order to complete an activity.

- **ESL students have varied needs and interests.**
  Each activity in *Classic Classroom Activities* is <u>self-contained</u>, allowing you to pick and choose the topics and vocabulary most relevant to your students. You may also choose to teach the units sequentially.

- **Listening, speaking, reading and writing, as well as grammar, phonetics and vocabulary should not be taught in isolation.**
  Classic Classroom Activities links essential vocabulary to these four skills. Your students improve their linguistic competency as they work cooperatively to locate and record information, act out a situation, listen to and give opinions, and even play games.

- **Visuals help students learn new language.**
  The activity pages feature clear, engaging art providing context that supports interesting student-centered tasks. Content-based Picture Cards (64 in each unit) provide hands-on, manipulative practice.

- **Most teachers need activities for multilevel classrooms.**
  Classic Classroom Activities devotes a separate section to multilevel applications in the **TEACHER'S NOTES**. Specific suggestions assist teachers who have one or more Beginning–Low, Beginning–High, and/or Intermediate–Low students. These multilevel applications enable you to make the activity easier or more challenging and to vary the degree of student independence.

2. WHAT'S IN THIS BOOK AND HOW IS IT ORGANIZED?

- **12 Topic-Based Units**
  The topics and vocabulary utilized in *Classic Classroom Activities* correspond to the 12 thematic units in *The Oxford Picture Dictionary*. These topics feature practical, essential vocabulary that students need to learn for their everyday communicative tasks at school, in the workplace, and at home.

- **11 Teacher's Notes**
  Teacher's Notes provide essential information for setting up, conducting, and extending each of the 10 activity types, as well as for the activities which correspond to the Picture Cards. Step-by-step instructions for conducting an activity, variations for multilevel classes, and helpful tips, are included for each activity.

- **10 Activity Types**
  The 4 activities featured in every unit are:

Round Table Label	Take a Stand
Role Play	Board Game

  The remaining 6 activities which are rotated throughout the units are:

Mixer	Drawing Dictation
Survey	Information Exchange
Picture Differences	Double Crossword

- **768 Reproducible Picture Cards**
  Every unit in *Classic Classroom Activities* contains four pages of topic-related Picture Cards, with 16 pictures on each page. These cards are preceded by a Picture Card Activities page, which provides directions for four activities using the Picture Card pages. In addition, one page of Picture Cards is used in the Board Game activity featured in every unit.

- **A Blank Grid (for use with the Picture Cards)**
  The grid is located on page 197. Directions for using the grid with the Picture Cards are found on the Picture Card Activities page in every unit.

- **An Activity Index**

  The index, on pages 198-200, is organized by activity type, providing quick access to a particular activity's page number.

3. HOW DO I USE *CLASSIC CLASSROOM ACTIVITIES?*

Before beginning an activity with your class, review one of the 11 TEACHER'S NOTES located on pages xii–xxii. To get started, read the **Activity Objective** to discover the purpose of the activity, and the **Before Class** section to learn how to prepare for the activity. In addition, read the information in the upper right-hand corner of the page on how to group students, how much time to allow for each activity, and which levels are most suited for a particular activity type.

Next, read the directions for either **QUICK START** or **STEP-BY-STEP**. **QUICK START** condenses the preview, presentation, and practice stages of a classroom activity into three easy steps (useful for teachers who are familiar with the activity type). **STEP-BY-STEP** contains more detailed, numbered steps for the activity, including specific ways to <u>review</u> the topic and target vocabulary, strategies to <u>model</u> the activity, and ways to <u>practice</u> the activity before students begin to work on the activity on their own. The **Hot Tip** section offers suggestions for making the activity simpler or more challenging, and tips for troubleshooting problems that may arise during the activity.

Finally, read **FOR MULTILEVEL CLASSES** which contains specific suggestions to enable you to customize the activity to your students' language levels:
Group 1— Beginning–Low,
Group 2— Beginning–High,
Group 3— Intermediate–Low.

4. WHAT TYPES OF REPRODUCIBLE ACTIVITIES ARE INCLUDED IN THE BOOK?

The chart below lists the reproducible activity types found in *Classic Classroom Activities*. These activities

Activity	Grouping	Description
Round-Table Label	Small Groups	Students work cooperatively to label pictured vocabulary items and check their accuracy.
Survey	Small Groups	Students ask and answer questions about personal preferences and work individually to record the results on a graph.
Mixer	Whole Class	Students get acquainted as they ask and answer yes/no questions with six classmates and write the responses on an activity sheet.
Information Exchange	Pairs	An information gap activity where students ask and answer questions to the answers on complementary activity sheets and then work together to check their accuracy.
Double Crossword	Pairs	Students ask for and give clues to solve a crossword puzzle and then work together to check their work.
Picture Differences	Pairs	Students study two almost identical scenes and work together to identify and list the differences on a chart.
Drawing Dictation	Pairs	Students take turns describing and drawing pictures according to their partners' directions.
Role Play	Small Groups	Students read and assign roles in topic-related conversations, create original dialog, and act out a situation.
Take a Stand	Pairs	Students read and analyze topic statements, choose a "pro" or "con" position, create original statements and discuss their opinions.
Board Game	Small Groups	Students play a game to review previously learned vocabulary taken from an entire unit.

are appropriate to all levels with the exception of Role Play and Take a Stand which work best in Beginning-High or Intermediate-Low classes.

Each activity is self-contained, so you may randomly choose any activity in the unit, or you can work sequentially within each unit. Within each unit, the activities are ordered from easy to more challenging in terms of student task and participation. Therefore, for example, you will always find Round Table Label as the first activity in each unit. The only departure from this progression is the Board Game, which is placed after the other activities where it can be utilized as a review and/or evaluation of the vocabulary students have learned in the unit. (See chart on page viii for this progression.)

5. HOW DO I USE THE PICTURE CARDS?

Before using the Picture Cards, read the TEACHER'S NOTES for the Picture Card Activities and Picture Cards on page xxii for an overview of how to use the Picture Cards, a description of the activities, and helpful hints for creating new activities.

There are seven Picture Card activities rotated throughout the 12 units, which include: PICK A PAIR, TWIN GRIDS, PEER DICTATION, NOW AND THEN CHARADES, MIXER, GUESS WHAT?, and PICK AND CHOOSE. Every unit contains four activities, one for each page of the Picture Cards. Step-by-step teacher directions for all four Picture Card activities in each unit are combined onto one Picture Card Activities page. Although they are located at the end of the unit (immediately after the Picture Card Activities page), the Picture Cards may be used any time additional vocabulary practice is needed. For some activities, students use the entire Picture Card page as a worksheet. Others have students cut the cards apart. (For tips on organizing and storing Picture Cards, see **TEACHING TIPS AND CLASSROOM MANAGEMENT STRATEGIES** below.)

TEACHING TIPS AND CLASSROOM MANAGEMENT STRATEGIES

Assembling and Storing Materials
Reproducible Activity Sheets
Before beginning any activity, make sure you check the **BEFORE CLASS** section at the top of the TEACHER'S NOTES. Do this _before_ you start duplicating a class set of activity sheets! Many of the activities are for pair or group work, and do not require individual copies of the materials. Also, gather all the materials you will need, such as manila folders, for the activity.

Picture Cards
How you assemble and organize your Picture Cards depends greatly on how you choose to use them in your classroom. You can have students color the Picture Card pages and then laminate them. You can duplicate entire class sets of Picture Card pages and store them, with or without the accompanying Word List. One of the Picture Card activities, PEER DICTATION, for example, requires student pairs to work only with pictures and then to check their spelling against the Word List. You can store the cut-apart Picture Cards in class sets of envelopes or have students create their own storage pockets by stapling half-sheets of construction paper to both sides of manila folders. These pocket folders of manipulatives can then be taken home for student practice or kept in a file box in the classroom.

Props
The Role Play activity calls for props, or real objects, to help set the stage and bring the activity to life. You can provide these materials (storing them in the classroom if you have space) or consider asking students to bring something in. Telling students about the activity a few days beforehand will build anticipation and provide time to allow them to collect what they need to bring from home.

FACILITATING THE ACTIVITY

Checking Comprehension
Classic Classroom Activities is not designed to teach the meaning of new vocabulary. It is crucial that students understand both the vocabulary on the activity page and the directions for the activity. Every activity page gives the _Dictionary_ page number(s) for the vocabulary used in the activity. If necessary, review and practice these words with your students before you begin the activity. To ensure that the activities run smoothly, all the TEACHER'S NOTES contain a specific technique for checking your students' comprehension of the directions.

Grouping Strategies
The act of grouping students in pairs or small groups is a communicative activity in itself. The way students are grouped facilitates their speaking practice by reducing first-language interference and non-participation. Ideally, have students work in mixed-language groups. Since this is not always possible, have students form mixed-ability or mixed-gender groups.

Since many activities involve student pairs, it is a good idea to encourage students to work with as many different people as possible. You can manipulate the distribution of the cards, giving specific cards to higher-level students, one language group, or one gender.

- Hand out playing cards and have students with the same numbers find each other.

- Distribute Picture Cards to half the class and word cards you've created using the blank grid on page 197 to the other half. Have students match pictures with words to form pairs.

Small group activities are most successful when group members have certain responsibilities. Possibilities include recorder, timekeeper, reporter, reader, English monitor, and observer. Alternate allowing students to form their own groups, assigning students into specific groups, or forming groups at random. To form groups:

- Take some time to mentally identify the homogeneous groups in your class (languages, ages, levels). Distribute one kind of card to each group. (All Spanish speakers get #1 or A, all Armenian speakers get #2 or B, etc.) Have students form groups of four *different* numbers or letters.

- Make name cards ahead of time and place them on the desks for "pre-assigned" groups. This works well if you have regularly attending students.

- Cut magazine pictures into four separate pieces, randomly distribute them, and have students "reassemble" the pictures to form their groups.

Monitoring
Your most important role during every activity is being aware of what's going on while students are doing the activity. This is the best time to assess how the activity is progressing and if it is meeting your students' needs. Walk around as unobtrusively as possible, make mental or actual notes of where students are having difficulty, listen for grammar and pronunciation problems, and "jump in" if students need you. All the TEACHER'S NOTES contain a monitoring reminder in the step-by-step directions.

Time Limits and Quiet Signals
Students need to know the parameters of a communicative task, including the time it takes to complete it. (The TEACHER'S NOTES suggest how much time an activity might take.) The use of a quiet signal to get the attention of the class helps students shift gears between the stages of an activity. Try these "attention grabbers" and make sure to vary them so they retain their punch: flick the lights on and off, ring a bell, blow a whistle, raise your hand, wave a flag. Once time has been called, students need to focus on the **What's next?** activity at the bottom of the page.

USING THE OVERHEAD PROJECTOR (OHP)
Teachers fortunate enough to have OHPs in their classrooms will find overhead transparencies very helpful. Here are some suggestions for using transparencies:

- Make a transparency of the activity and use it *before* distributing your class set. By masking sections with blank paper, you can focus students' attention on just a portion of the sheet while you set up the activity. You or a student volunteer can write directly on the transparency to model the activity.

- Play Concentration with the whole class to reinforce vocabulary. Make a transparency of the blank grid on page 197. Write the letters A-D across the top of the grid and number the boxes 1-4 down the left of the grid. Make a transparency of a selected Picture Card page and cut apart the pictures. Choose 8 pictures and place them in the boxes in the top two rows of the grid. In the remaining squares, write the corresponding words. Using 16 small squares of paper, mask each of the squares on the entire grid. Have students take turns calling out two squares (*A2* and *B4*), trying to match the picture and the word.

- Transparencies of *The Oxford Picture Dictionary* pages are available and are useful for reviewing an activity's target vocabulary and/or providing additional vocabulary practice.

Teacher's Notes

ROUND TABLE LABEL

Activity Objective: Students take turns identifying and labeling the target vocabulary in a scene, then work together to check the accuracy of the completed activity sheet.

Before Class: Duplicate one selected Round Table Label activity sheet for each group of four.

Groups of 4
25 minutes
Beginning, Intermediate–Low

QUICK START

Ready...

Draw an apple on the board and label it. Next, draw a strawberry on the board and label it an orange. Ask your students to correct your work. When they tell you how to label the picture, ask them how to spell the word.

Set...

Distribute the activity sheet and review the directions. Model the labeling activity by having one group take turns passing the sheet from student to student, writing their names at the top of the paper.

Go!...

Have one student in each group label one item on the sheet and pass it to the next student. Students should help one another, but only the student who has the paper should write on it. The activity ends when all items are labeled. Groups look at the *Dictionary* to check their work.

STEP-BY-STEP

1. Draw an apple on the board and label it. Next, draw a strawberry on the board and label it an orange. Ask your students to correct your work. When they tell you how to label the picture, ask them how to spell the word. Make mistakes and correct them. This shows your students how to help one another complete the activity sheet.
2. Show students one copy of the activity sheet and tell them that they will be working in groups, taking turns labeling the items on the activity sheet.
3. Have students form groups of four and number off within their groups, #1-#4.
4. Have each #1 come to you and pick up the copy of the activity sheet for his or her group.
5. Review the directions on the sheet and check students' comprehension by asking yes/no questions.

Do you use your Dictionary *to help label the pictures?* [no] *Do you write all the words when you get the paper?* [no] *Do you pass the paper to the person next to you?* [yes]

6. Have the #1's label one item on the sheet and check their accuracy with their group. Circulate to see if everyone is working together.
7. Have the groups continue labeling and passing the sheet around the group. Monitor their progress and encourage students to ask their group members for help if they are unsure of a word or its spelling.
8. Have students check their completed sheets against the appropriate *Dictionary* pages and make any necessary corrections.
9. Do the **What's next?** activity with the class.

Hot Tip: Be sure students are sitting close enough to each other to interact and to pass and see the paper with ease.

FOR MULTILEVEL CLASSES

GROUP 1 — Beginning–Low   GROUP 2 — Beginning–High   GROUP 3 — Intermediate–Low

GROUP 1 – Work with the teacher and label the scene on the overhead projector.
GROUP 2 – Complete the activity sheet in small groups.
GROUP 3 – Complete the activity sheet and then take turns writing sentences about each item.

TEACHER'S NOTES: **MIXER**

Whole Class
35 minutes
Beginning, Intermediate–Low

Activity Objective: Students complete missing information on an activity sheet and randomly circulate, asking and answering questions using their activity sheets as cues.

Before Class: Duplicate the selected Mixer activity sheet for each student.

QUICK START

Ready…

Write a yes/no question on the board, marking a blank space for each letter in the target word. Draw a picture cue for the word and have students fill in the letters. Ask several students and write their names under "yes" or "no" when they answer.

Set…

Distribute the activity sheet and review the direction lines. Practice the first question, helping students fill in the missing information. Have individual students complete the missing information for the remaining questions. Then model the activity by taking turns asking and answering the first question with one student.

Go!…

Have students circulate to complete their activity sheets. Enter the mixer yourself to monitor student's progress. Students sit down when their activity sheet is complete.

STEP-BY-STEP

1. Write a sample yes/no question on the board. Make a blank line for each letter of the target word, (Do you waer g_ _ _ _ _ _?) and have students fill in the missing letters. Draw a picture cue for the word. Draw two boxes under the question and write "yes" in one and "no" in the other.
2. Ask students the question and, according to their answers, write the students' first names in the appropriate yes and no boxes.
3. Distribute the activity sheet and review the directions. Model the activity by helping the class complete the first question. Write the missing letters on the board.
4. Have students work individually to complete the missing information for the remaining questions.
5. Check students' comprehension of the activity by asking yes/no questions. Do you answer the questions yourself? [no] Do you have students write their names on your activity sheet? [no] Do you fill

in both the yes and no boxes? [yes]
6. Invite two volunteers to the front. Student A asks the first question and Student B responds. Student A writes Student B's first name in the appropriate answer box, clarifying spelling if necessary. *(Katya – is the first letter K or C?)* Point out that students must talk to at least two different classmates, if possible, to complete both yes and no boxes for each question.
7. Have students stand up and circulate to find answers for all the questions on their activity sheets. Monitor student practice by walking around and checking papers. Students will enjoy your participating in the mixer yourself and you can check their verbal and spelling accuracy directly.
8. Students can stay "in the mix" and help others when their activity sheet is complete.
9. Do the **What's next?** activity with the class.

Hot Tip: Move desks and chairs out of the way to create a "mixing" area in the center of the room. Students are more likely to talk with a greater number of people if they have space to walk around in.

FOR MULTILEVEL CLASSES

GROUP 1 — Beginning–Low   GROUP 2 — Beginning–High   GROUP 3 — Intermediate–Low

Group 1 – Work with the teacher to complete the activity sheet.

Group 2 – Complete the activity sheet individually.

Group 3 – Complete the activity and then write several sentences about your classmates and share them with a partner.

TEACHER'S NOTES: **SURVEY**

Activity Objective: Students ask and answer classmates' questions about personal preference, then work individually to record the results on a graph.

Before Class: Duplicate the selected Survey activity sheet for each student.

QUICK START

Ready…

Write a personal preference question on the board e.g., *Do you prefer coffee or tea?* and answer it yourself by marking a check in a column chart. Ask a student the same question: *Jorge, do you prefer coffee or tea?* and mark the response. Repeat for three more students. Transfer the results of all five responses to the bar graph on the page.

Set…

Distribute the activity sheet and review the directions. Model the survey activity by having one student read and answer the first question and then ask nine other students the same question. Chart all responses on the board.

Go!…

Have students first answer all the survey questions themselves, and then walk around, interviewing nine other students to complete their charts. Have students return to their seats to complete the activity sheet, transferring the information on their chart to a graph. The activity ends after students discuss and write about their survey results.

STEP BY STEP

1. Write a personal preference question on the board, for example, *Do you prefer coffee or tea?* Answer it yourself by marking a check in a column chart. Then ask and record the responses of three more students.

2. Draw a sample bar graph on the board, marking the vertical axis with the numbers 1-5 and placing one bar showing the two separate responses to the sample question on the horizontal axis. Point out that there is no place to transfer the *no opinion* column on the checklist.

3. Show students one copy of the activity sheet and tell them that they will be asking and answering opinion questions about a topic and recording the results on a chart and on a graph.

4. Review the directions on the sheet and check students' comprehension of the activity by asking

yes/no questions. *Do you answer all the question yourself first?* [yes] *Do you ask another students to record information on the bar graph?* [no]

5. Have students complete the survey questions themselves. When they are finished, have them get up and walk around, interviewing nine other students to complete their grids. Circulate to make sure students are marking responses correctly.

6. Have students return to their seats to complete the second half of the activity sheet, transferring the information on their chart to the bar graph. Remind students that they do not record the "No opinion" information on the graph.

7. Walk around, checking students' completed bar graph results against their charts, making sure that the numbers match.

8. Do the **What's next?** activity with the class.

Hot Tip: Review and practice ways for students to express their opinions and talk about their graph results. *I prefer to drive a taxi. 7 out of 10 students prefer driving a truck.*

FOR MULTILEVEL CLASSES

GROUP 1 — Beginning–Low   GROUP 2 — Beginning–High   GROUP 3 — Intermediate–Low

Group 1 – Work in groups of four, completing identical graphs.

Group 2 – Complete the activity sheet and then report the findings in small groups.

Group 3 – Complete the activity sheet and then create four more survey questions on the topic. Arrange to have your students interview another class and compare both classes' results.

TEACHER'S NOTES: **DRAWING DICTATION**

Pairs
30 minutes
Beginning, Intermediate–Low

Activity Objective: Student pairs take turns describing pictures and drawing them according to their partners' directions.

Before Class: Duplicate half a class set of each page of the selected Drawing Dictation activity sheets and collect half a class set of manila folders to be used as screens.

QUICK START

Ready...
Place several classroom objects on a table and draw a blank table on the board. Ask students to describe the table items and their location so that you can draw each one on the board. Make intentional mistakes and have students correct you. *No, the pen is next to the* <u>notebook</u>.

Set...
Have students form pairs, and distribute the "A" and "B" Drawing Dictation activity sheets and manila folders. Students set up the folders between themselves as screens. Review the directions and the clarification questions. Model the Drawing Dictation by having one student pair describe and draw one item on the activity sheet.

Go!...
Have student pairs take turns describing and drawing pictures. The activity ends when both pictures are complete. Have pairs remove the screens and compare their work.

STEP-BY-STEP

1. Arrange several classroom objects on a table and have students describe each item so that you can draw on the board.
2. Model the language and clarification strategy you want students to use in the activity. Ask one student to come to the board and draw the items you describe. *Draw a round dinner plate in the center. Now, put a napkin on the left side of the plate.* Switch roles and have students tell you where to draw items. Discuss different clarification strategies, such as *Did you say on the left or right? Did you say napkin?*
3. Tell students that they will take turns describing and drawing different pictures with a partner.
4. Have students form pairs and assign each an "A" or "B" role. Distribute one manila folder to each pair. Show how to prop the folders up between partners as a screen. Tell the pairs they will take turns dictating and drawing.

5. Distribute the "A" and "B" activity sheets to the appropriate partners. Review the direction lines. Check for comprehension by asking "A" students in activity #1, *Do you draw a picture for your partner?* [no] *Do you answer your partner's questions?* [yes] Ask the "B" students in activity #1, *Do you write the words you hear in the picture?* [no] *Do you ask your partner questions?* [yes]
6. Have one student pair demonstrate the activity for the class. One student describes one item in the drawing while the other listens and draws what s/he hears.
7. Have student pairs complete activity #1 and then complete activity #2. Monitor by walking around to check on students' progress and help with clarification questions.
8. Have students check their completed activity sheets by removing their screens and comparing them.
9. Do the **What's next?** activity with the class.

Hot Tip: A perfect drawing is not the goal. Distributing markers or crayons may "loosen up" students and encourage them to have fun while they learn.

FOR MULTILEVEL CLASSES

GROUP 1 — Beginning–Low   GROUP 2 — Beginning–High   GROUP 3 — Intermediate–Low

Group 1 - Use only the "A" activity sheet and draw items that the teacher describes.

Group 2 - Complete the "A" and "B" activity sheets in pairs.

Group 3 - Describe the items to their partners <u>without</u> saying the target word. *You drink coffee or tea from this. Draw it on the left side of the table.* [cup]

TEACHER'S NOTES: **PICTURE DIFFERENCES**

Activity Objective: Student pairs study two almost identical scenes together in order to uncover differences between the two pictures.

Before Class: Duplicate half a class set of each page of the selected Picture Differences activity sheets.

Pairs
30 minutes
Beginning, Intermediate–Low

QUICK START

Ready...
Draw two separate pictures on the board showing one difference, for example, Picture A: happy face with short hair/Picture B: sad face with short hair. Ask students, *What's the difference?* and write their responses under each picture on the board.

Set...
Have students form pairs and distribute the appropriate activity sheets. Review the directions and have students find and point to the sample picture difference on their activity sheets. This difference is written on both students' charts.

Go!...
Have student pairs look at their pictures together, search for the differences and complete their own charts. The activity ends when all 10 picture differences have been discovered.

STEP-BY-STEP

1. Draw two separate pictures on the board showing one difference. [Picture A: a happy face with short hair, Picture B: a sad face with short hair), or use classroom objects such as two notebooks, one open and the other closed. Ask students, *What's the difference?* Model the correct language students will need to do the activity. *Picture A has a happy face. Picture B has a sad face.* Write their short answer responses on the board in two columns— column A: happy face, column B: sad face.

2. Have students form pairs and assign each an "A" or "B" role. Distribute the "A" and "B" activity sheets to the appropriate partners. Tell students that each partner will have a paper with an almost identical scene. Explain that they will be looking together at both pictures to find and record the differences.

3. Review the directions and check for comprehension of the activity. Ask yes/no questions such as, *Do you look at each other's pictures?* [yes] *Do you write your answers on one chart?* [no]

4. Review prepositions vocabulary that students might need to find the picture differences in the scenes. *In my picture, there's a sign on the left side. Is there a sign in your picture? What's on the top of your picture?*

5. Have students cover the charts on the bottom of their activity sheets. Ask the "A" students to locate the sample item in their pictures (listed as picture difference #1 on both the "A" and "B" charts) *Do you see a laundry basket? Where is it? Is it full or empty?* Ask "B" students the same question.

6. Have all the pairs examine their pictures, discuss the differences and write them on their charts. Monitor by walking around to check on students' progress and help with any language difficulties.

7. Have students use their *Dictionaries* to check their spelling after they have finished recording the picture differences.

8. When all the pairs have finished, survey their results with the class. Elicit the picture differences they have found and write them on the board.

9. Do the **What's next?** activity with the class.

Hot Tip: Make transparencies of "A" and "B" pictures and have student volunteers circle the picture differences. See Using the Overhead Projector, page x.

FOR MULTILEVEL CLASSES

GROUP 1 — Beginning–Low GROUP 2 —Beginning–High GROUP 3 — Intermediate–Low

Group 1 - Students work with the teacher to find the picture differences.

Group 2 - Student pairs work together to find and record the picture differences.

Group 3 - Using a manila folder as a screen between pairs, students find and record the picture differences without looking at each others' activity sheets.

TEACHER'S NOTES: **DOUBLE CROSSWORD**

Pairs

30 minutes

Beginning,
Intermediate–Low

Activity Objective: Student pairs take turns giving and receiving clues in order to complete a crossword puzzle.

Before Class: Duplicate half a class set of each page of the selected Double Crossword activity sheets. Collect half a class set of manila folders to be used as screens.

QUICK START

Ready…
Write a sample clue on the board. Draw blank squares for each letter in the target word and fill in one letter. Ask students, *What's the word?,* and fill in the letters.

Set…
Have students form pairs and distribute the "A" and "B" Double Crossword activity sheets and manila folders. Students set up the folders between themselves as screens. Review the direction lines. Model the activity by having one *A* student give a clue from the puzzle and one B student write the answer on the *B* activity sheet.

Go!…
Have students complete the crossword puzzle and check their answers by comparing their activity sheets.

STEP-BY-STEP

1. Write a sample clue on the board: *You write with this.* Draw six connected blank squares, filling the letter "p" in the first square. Have a student read you the clue and fill in the remaining letters for <u>pencil</u>. Ask clarification questions such as, *Is the fourth letter a "c" or an "s"?*
2. Repeat with another clue: *You write on this.* Have a volunteer student come up and fill in the remaining letters for *paper.*
3. Tell students that they will take turns giving and receiving clues for missing words in order to complete their crossword puzzles.
4. Have students form pairs and assign each an "A" or "B" role. Distribute a manila folder to each pair. Show how to prop the folders up between partners as screens.
5. Distribute the "A" and "B" activity sheets to the appropriate partners. Review the direction lines. Check for comprehension by asking, *Do you show your partner your paper?* [no] *Do you read all the*

clues to your partner at the same time? [no]

6. Have one student pair demonstrate the activity for the class, with Student A reading the first down clue for Student B, and Student B reading the first across clue for Student A.
7. Have students take turns reading all the clues and filling in the words to complete their puzzles. Monitor student practice by walking around to check on students' progress. Encourage students to ask for clarification if they don't understand their partners' clue words or spelling. *Did you say 2 across or 3 across? Was that a B or a V?*
8. Have students check their answers by removing the screens and comparing their completed crossword puzzles. If you're using an overhead projector, make transparencies of both the A and B activity sheets. Have "A" students come up and fill in the horizontal words, and "B" students fill in the vertical words.
9. Do the **What's next?** activity with the class.

Hot Tip: Review pronunciation of consonants by practicing minimal pairs (<u>b</u>at-<u>v</u>at, <u>l</u>ock-<u>r</u>ock) and teach techniques for identifying letters, e.g., E *as in* egg, A *as in* apple.

FOR MULTILEVEL CLASSES

GROUP 1 — Beginning–Low   GROUP 2 — Beginning–High   GROUP 3 — Intermediate–Low

Group 1 - Use only the "A" activity sheet and complete the puzzle with the teacher.

Group 2 - Complete the "A" and "B" activity sheets in pairs.

Group 3 - Complete the activity sheet and write additional clues for the topic, connecting the new words to the crossword puzzle. New words may extend beyond the original puzzle grid.

TEACHER'S NOTES: **INFORMATION EXCHANGE**

Pairs
30 minutes
Beginning, Intermediate–Low

Activity Objective: Student pairs ask and answer questions to complete different activity sheets, then work together to check the accuracy of the completed information.

Before Class: Duplicate half a class set of each page of the selected Information Exchange activity sheet and collect half a class set of manila folders to be used as screens.

QUICK START

Ready...	**Set...**	**Go!...**
Write on the board and model a sample question or statement that students will need for the activity. Substitute vocabulary students will use and practice clarification questions.	Have students form pairs. Distribute the "A" and "B" Information Exchange sheets and manila folders. Students set up the folders between themselves as screens. Practice a sample question from the "A" and "B" sheets with the whole class.	Have students ask each other questions to fill in the missing information on their activity sheets. They then check their accuracy by comparing their completed papers.

STEP-BY-STEP

1. Review the vocabulary students need for the Information Exchange. Write several sentences on the board that relate to the topic and have students practice answering questions about the words you underline: Mix two cups of <u>flour</u> and 1/2 cup <u>raisins</u>. *How much flour do you need? How many raisins do you use?*

2. Have students substitute different vocabulary words for the underlined words and continue asking and answering questions. Discuss different clarification strategies, such as, *Excuse me? Did you say one or two cups of flour? How many raisins was that?*

3. Tell students that they will take turns asking for and giving missing information in order to complete different activity sheets.

4. Have students form pairs and assign each an "A" or "B" role. Distribute one manila folder to each pair.

Show students how to prop the folders up between partners as screens.

5. Distribute the "A" and "B" activity sheets to the appropriate partners. Review the direction lines. Check for comprehension by asking "A" students a question that only they will be able to answer. Do the same for "B" students.

6. Have one student pair demonstrate the activity for the class by having A ask B a question and B write the answer on the B activity sheet.

7. Have students ask and answer the questions to complete their activity sheets. Monitor student practice by walking around to check on students' progress and help with clarification questions.

8. Have students check their answers by removing their screens and comparing activity sheets.

9. Do the **What's Next?** activity with the class.

Hot Tip: Pair students with different ability levels to promote mentoring, and with different languages to encourage students to speak English.

FOR MULTILEVEL CLASSES

GROUP 1 — Beginning–Low   GROUP 2 — Beginning–High   GROUP 3 — Intermediate–Low

Group 1 - Use only the "A" activity sheet and write in target vocabulary as the teacher dictates.

Group 2 - Complete the "A" and "B" activity sheets in pairs.

Group 3 - Complete the activity sheet. Then work together to create an original recipe, schedule, or informational flyer using the target vocabulary in the activity.

TEACHER'S NOTES: **ROLE PLAY**

Small Groups

60 minutes

Beginning–High
Intermediate–Low

Activity Objective: Students working in groups read and assign roles in a topic-related conversation and act out a role play.

Before Class: Duplicate the selected Role Play activity sheet for each student. Look at the <u>Script</u> to determine the target vocabulary required to do the activity and look at the <u>Props</u> to determine what items you need to collect.

QUICK START

Ready...
Write the Role Play scene and characters on the board and have students predict what conversations they might hear.

Set...
Have students form groups. Distribute the activity sheets and props. Review the directions, practice saying one or two lines from the script, and have students identify the speaker.

Go!...
Have students choose a character, practice the lines, and act out the Role Play with the group.

STEP-BY-STEP

1. Review the vocabulary students need for the Role Play. Write the Role Play setting, e.g., a hair salon and two characters on the board, e.g., customer and hair stylist. Write a sentence for each character and ask students to identify the speaker.

2. Have students substitute different vocabulary for each sentence and practice saying the lines. *I want <u>curly</u> hair. (<u>straight, brown, wavy,</u> etc.)* Ask students to tell you other lines that the characters might say. Write these lines on the board.

3. Tell students they will be reading a script, deciding which persons are speaking, and then acting out the characters and situation in a group.

4. Distribute the Role Play activity sheets to each student. Distribute or display the props for the class to see.

5. Have students form groups of four. [See **Grouping Strategies**, pages ix-x.] Review the direction lines. Check for comprehension of the activity by asking questions such as, *Do you complete the activity*

sheet by yourself? [no] *Do you say the lines out loud?* [yes]

6. Set a time limit (10-15 minutes) for the groups to read the script and decide which character is speaking each line. Have students write the characters' names on the spaces provided on the activity sheet. Call time and ask different students to read each line and identify the speaker.

7. Invite two group members to the front. Have them each pick a line of dialog from the script and act it out for the class. Encourage students to improvise and change the words in italics to create new lines. Write these lines on the board.

8. Have all the groups act out the role play in their groups. Monitor student practice by walking around and helping with pronunciation problems such as register, stress and intonation. Encourage pantomime and improvisation.

9. Do the **What's next?** activity with the class.

Hot Tip: Cut up related Picture Cards for students to use as cues in creating a Role Play. If you have access to a video camera, record the Role Plays and play them back for the students to enjoy and evaluate. Take a class vote on the funniest, most creative, etc.

FOR MULTILEVEL CLASSES

NOTE: *This activity is not recommended for* GROUP 1 — Beginning–Low

GROUP 2 — Beginning–High

GROUP 3 — Intermediate–Low

Group 2 - Complete the Role Play and perform the "drama" in small groups.

Group 3 - Complete the Role Play in small groups and perform the "drama" for the whole class. Other students can help draw scenery and props.

TEACHER'S NOTES: **TAKE A STAND**

Activity Objective: Students read and analyze topic statements for a pro or con position and discuss their own opinions with partners.

Before Class: Duplicate a class set of the selected Take a Stand activity sheet. Assemble realia, newspaper or magazine articles, or pictures that illustrate both positions. Look over statements A-J on the activity sheet to determine which topic vocabulary students may need to review.

Pairs
45 minutes
Beginning – High Intermediate – Low

QUICK START

Ready…

Write the topic question on the board and discuss it with the whole class. Read a sample statement and survey the class to find out which position they think it supports.

Set…

Distribute the Take a Stand activity sheet and review the directions. Go over unfamiliar vocabulary and discuss the first statement with the whole class.

Go!…

Have students complete the activity sheet individually, then find partners to compare papers with and write their ideas about the topic.

STEP-BY-STEP

1. Introduce the topic by writing the activity title on the board and discussing it. Ask several related questions, e.g., for home-cooked meals/fast food *Do you like to eat at home? How often do you eat in restaurants? What's your favorite fast food?*

2. Read a sample statement and survey the class to find out which position they think it supports. Have students brainstorm vocabulary that relates to both positions and write these words on the board, e.g., *fast food - inexpensive, fast, take-out, etc.*

3. Tell students they will read statements to determine whether they represent a "for" or "against" position and write their own ideas about the topic.

4. Distribute the activity sheets. Review the direction lines. Check for comprehension of the activity by asking questions such as, *Can you check both*

columns? [no] *Can you use your* Dictionary *to look up words you don't know?* [yes]

5. Read the first statement with the class and have students decide which column they should check.

6. Set a time limit (10-15 minutes) for students to work individually, reading statements A–J and making checks in the appropriate columns.

7. Have students pair up to compare their papers and to write two additional topic statements. Students then write their ideas and their partner's ideas about the topic. Monitor student progress by walking around to help with students' conversation and writing.

8. Do the **What's next?** activity with the class.

Hot Tip: Teach students the meaning of "Pro" and "Con." Make sure they have ample time to practice new vocabulary in context before doing the Take a Stand activity.

FOR MULTILEVEL CLASSES

GROUP 2 — Beginning–High   GROUP 3 — Intermediate–Low

Note: This activity is not recommended for Group 1, Beginning–Low.

Group 2 - Complete the activity sheet as a whole class, then act as an audience as group 3 debates the topic.

Group 3 - Complete the activity sheet individually and in pairs; then have two pairs of students conduct a debate on the topic, choosing opposing sides and presenting their positions to the class.

TEACHER'S NOTES: **BOARD GAME**

Activity Objective: Students playing a game in teams, ask and answer questions, draw, and respond to commands in order to practice previously learned topic vocabulary.

Before Class: Duplicate the selected Board Game activity sheets for each group of four and tape the sheets together to form the game boards. Duplicate one page of the selected Picture Cards for each group. Each game board identifies the picture cards needed to play. Assemble scrap paper, coins, and scissors. Draw a simple version of three Picture Cards on large sheets of paper or duplicate and enlarge them to use as examples.

QUICK START

Ready…
Copy the first four squares of the activity sheet on the board. Place the three large Picture Cards face down and use student volunteers to demonstrate placing a marker, flipping a coin to move forward, and responding to the commands on the game board.

Set…
Distribute one game board and one set of the designated picture card page to each group of four students. Pass out scrap paper, scissors and coins. Have students prepare materials and review the directions on the game board.

Go!…
Have students play the game while you circulate and serve as a "referee" to monitor the activity. The activity ends when all students reach "Finish" on the board game.

STEP-BY-STEP

1. Discuss games that students have played. Talk about rules, taking turns, game boards, markers, and flipping a coin. Tell students that they will be playing a game to improve their vocabulary and spelling skills and to practice answering and asking questions.

2. Draw the first four squares of the activity sheet on the board or use a transparency of the first Board Game page. Place the three large Picture Cards face down.

3. Make a game marker by writing your first name on a small piece of paper and placing it on the "Start" star. Demonstrate flipping a coin and calling heads to move two spaces, tails to move one space, as you move your marker. Read and respond to the directions on the square. Get class consensus on its accuracy.

4. Use student volunteers to take two turns playing the sample game.

5. Have students form groups of four and number off within their groups, #1 – #4. Have the #1's come to

you and pick up their group's copy of the game board, the #2's get the Picture Card page, the #3's get the scissors, and the #4's get scrap paper and a coin.

6. Allow time for the groups to cut up and shuffle the picture cards and to make their markers.

7. Have students play the game while you circulate and "referee" the activity. You can also identify an advanced student to observe (forming a group of five) and referee the game, using the *Dictionary* to check spelling.

8. **What's next?**: Play a game with the whole class. Before class, write different commands and/or questions related to the board game topic on index cards. Form two teams and have all students stand. Students take turns responding to the cards and sit down when they have answered correctly. Those who answer incorrectly continue standing to take another turn. The first team to be seated wins. (You can also award one point for each correct answer.)

Hot Tip: Emphasize the cooperative nature of this game by encouraging students to help each other; point out that the goal is for all group members to reach "Finish!"
Laminate the game boards and Picture Cards! You may want to use them again.

FOR MULTILEVEL CLASSES

GROUP 1 — Beginning–Low   GROUP 2 — Beginning–High   GROUP 3 — Intermediate–Low

Group 1 - Play the game in pairs with a group of three students or the teacher monitoring the activity.

Group 2 - Play the game in groups of four.

Group 3 - Play the game and then work in pairs to create new commands on index cards on the board game topic. Respond to these new commands with opposing student pairs.

TEACHER'S NOTES: **PICTURE CARD ACTIVITIES AND PICTURE CARDS**

WHAT ARE PICTURE CARDS?

Each *Classic Classroom Activity* unit features 64 Picture Cards arranged on four pages with 16 pictures per page. There is a referenced Word List on each Picture Card page. The majority of the Picture Cards within a unit depict words found in the corresponding unit of the *The Oxford Picture Dictionary;* in some cases, however, a few words from previous units are depicted in order to create more meaningful activities.

HOW DO I USE THE PICTURE CARDS?

There is a Picture Card Activities Page in each unit, preceding the four pages of Picture Cards. This page contains four separate Picture Card activities with step-by-step directions to help you easily set-up, model, and practice each one. Choose an activity, duplicate the Picture Card page referenced directly under the activity title, and follow the directions. There is one activity (Twin Grids) which requires a blank grid (page 197) in addition to the Picture Cards. This blank grid is useful, for both matching activities and creating word cards.

WHAT ARE THE PICTURE CARD ACTIVITIES?

The following seven Picture Card activities are rotated throughout the book:

Activity	Grouping	What is it?
Pick a Pair	pairs	matching card game
Twin Grids	pairs	matching grid game
Peer Dictation	pairs	information sharing
Now and Then Charades	small groups	information guessing (non-verbal clues), practice with past tense
Mixer	whole class	information search
Guess What?	small groups	information guessing (verbal clues)
Pick and Choose	small groups	decision making, categorizing

WHAT ELSE CAN I DO WITH THESE PICTURE CARDS?

There are numerous possibilities for other Picture Card activities. Here are some suggestions:

• *Flash Cards*

Flash Cards are especially helpful to Beginning students in improving their sight-word vocabulary. Distribute one Picture Card page to each student pair. Students can cut up the pictures and write the corresponding word on the reverse side of each Picture Card. Then students can work in pairs or groups; one student identifies each picture by saying it and spelling it while the other looks at the reverse side to verify accuracy.

• *Word Cards*

Word cards are useful for Intermediate students, who can cut apart the blank grid, write in vocabulary and arrange the words to create sentences and generate original stories. Using word cards in conjunction with the Picture Cards enables you to create activities for students at all levels. Make copies of the blank grid and a Picture Card page. Students can cut up both pages, write a word in each blank square to match each picture, and use both sets to play matching games.

• *Picture Card Dictionary*

Students can compile several Picture Card pages from any unit to create a personalized picture dictionary. Distribute one grid page of Picture Cards per student. [Cut off the Word List before duplicating the class set!] Students can work together to label the pictures of items they know, then go to their *Dictionaries* to complete the labeling and check their spelling. Once they have several completed pages, they can assemble their own picture dictionaries. An alternative use for individual Picture Card pages is to have students label a page independently as a spelling test for a unit. You can also make an overhead of a Picture Card page to use as a whole-class labeling activity or as an evaluation of learned vocabulary.

• *Verb Picture Cards*

Use Picture Cards featuring actions as cues for practicing verb tenses. Students can change a picture prompt such as, *Wash the dishes* to *Yesterday I washed the dishes* or *Tomorrow I'll wash the dishes.* Intermediate students can create sentences with modal and passive verb forms. *I should have washed the dishes. The dishes have already been washed.*

ENJOY THE ACTIVITIES AND REMEMBER: ONE PICTURE CARD IS WORTH A THOUSAND WORDS!

1. Everyday Language

Page(s)		A Classroom (2–3)	Personal Information (4)	School (5)	Studying (6–7)	Everyday Conversation (8)	The Telephone (9)	Weather (10)	Describing Things (11)	Colors (12)	Prepositions (13)	Numbers and Measurements (14–15)	Time (16–17)	The Calendar (18–19)	Money (20)	Shopping (21)
2	**Where's the pencil?** (Round Table Label)	◆									◆					
3	**Hello! Hola! ПРИВЕТ!** (Mixer)					◆										
4–5	**How much was that call to New York?** (Information Exchange)						◆					◆	◆	◆	◆	
6–7	**Numbers Puzzle** (Double Crossword)											◆				
8–9	**What's in her office?** (Drawing Dictation)	◆		◆					◆		◆					
10–11	**School Days** (Picture Differences)			◆					◆							
12	**Is it on sale?** (Role Play)								◆	◆					◆	◆
13	**Learn English at Home or at School?** (Take a Stand)			◆	◆											
14–15	**Everyday Language Board Game** (Board Game)	◆	◆	◆	◆	◆	◆	◆	◆	◆	◆	◆	◆	◆	◆	◆
16–20	**Picture Card Activities and Picture Cards**	◆		◆				◆		◆				◆	◆	

Where's the pencil?

The Oxford Picture Dictionary, pages 2–3, 13. See page xii for Teacher's Notes.

- ◆ Form groups of 4 people.
- ◆ Each person in the group takes turns labeling the classroom items on this paper.
- ◆ After all the pictures have labels, look in the *Dictionary* to check your group's work.

SOUTH AMERICA

Brazil

ABCDEFGHIJKLM
NOPQRSTUVWXYZ

Homework:
Ask three people about

student

- ◆ **What's next?** Your teacher will draw a desk with several open drawers on the chalkboard. Take turns telling student volunteers what to draw <u>on</u>, <u>in</u>, or <u>under</u> the desk drawers.

Hello! Hola! ПРИВЕТ!

The Oxford Picture Dictionary, page 8. See page xiii for Teacher's Notes.

◆ **Write the missing words on the lines.**

◆ **Walk around the room. Ask and answer the questions.**

◆ **Write a different name in each box.**

1. Can you say ___good___ ___morning___ in Spanish?

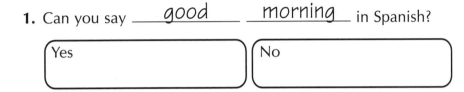

Yes	No

2. Can you say _____-_____ in French?

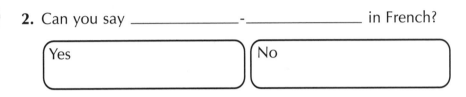

Yes	No

3. Can you say _____ _____ _____ in Chinese?

Yes	No

4. Can you say _____ _____ in Russian?

Yes	No

5. Can you say _____ _____ in Arabic?

Yes	No

6. Can you say _____ _____ in Korean?

Yes	No

◆ **What's next?** Share the different ways of greeting, thanking, and apologizing that you heard during the activity.

How much was that call to New York?

The Oxford Picture Dictionary, pages 9, 14–20. See page xviii for Teacher's Notes.

Information Exchange

A

1

- Sit with a partner. (Don't show this paper to your partner!)
- Ask your partner about the missing information on the phone bill below.
- You can use these questions:

   When did Eliza call _____ ?"

   "What time did Eliza make the call to _____ ?

   "How long was the call to _____ ?"

   "How much did the call to _____ cost?"

- Write in the missing information and read it back to your partner to check your work.

Eliza Oxford
1234 Elm Ave.
Pelham, NY

Account Number
(914) 555-9678

Statement Date
Apr. 14, 2003

BLUE BELL LONG-DISTANCE CALLS

•**Domestic**

Date	Time	Place and Number Called		Type	Rate	Minutes	Amount
Mar 13	5:10 PM	Fanfield, NJ	(906) 555-6896	Direct	_____	2	_____
_____	9:30 PM	Scottsdale, AZ	_____	Direct	Night	_____	.76
Mar 27	_____	Encino, CA	(818) 555-7803	Direct	_____	10	_____

•**International**

Date	Time	Place and Number Called		Type	Rate	Minutes	Amount
Mar 17	8:19 AM	Seoul, Korea	_____	Direct	Day	_____	2.12
_____	2:00 PM	Warsaw, Poland	(48) 22-555-7863	Direct	_____	6	_____

2

- Use the phone bill below to answer your partner's questions.

Patrick Jensen
5231 Oak Dr.
Encino, CA

Account Number
(818) 555-7803

Statement Date
Apr. 14, 2003

GTI

GTI LONG-DISTANCE CALLS

•**Domestic**

Date	Time	Place and Number Called		Type	Rate	Minutes	Amount
Mar 14	6:10 AM	Pelham, NY	(914) 555-9678	Direct	Day	5	2.49
Mar 15	3:30 PM	Seattle, WA	(206) 555-7145	Direct	Day	22	24.19
Mar 31	8:15 PM	Boulder, CO	(303) 555-3012	Direct	Day	3	3.04

•**International**

Date	Time	Place and Number Called		Type	Rate	Minutes	Amount
Mar 12	8:19 AM	London, GB	(44) 171-555-7000	Direct	Day	4	5.94
Mar 28	11:00 PM	Madrid, Spain	(34) 1-555-8204	Direct	Night	9	7.37

- **What's next?** Look at the time zone map on page 17 of the *Dictionary.* What time was it in each city when Eliza and Patrick made their calls? Who do you think they were calling?

How much was that call to New York?

The Oxford Picture Dictionary, pages 9, 14–20. See page xviii for Teacher's Notes.

Information Exchange

B

1

◆ **Sit with a partner. (Don't show this paper to your partner!)**

◆ **Use the phone bill below to answer your partner's questions.**

Eliza Oxford	Account Number	Statement Date
1234 Elm Ave.	(914) 555-9678	Apr. 14, 2003
Pelham, NY		

BLUE BELL LONG-DISTANCE CALLS

•Domestic

Date	Time	Place and Number Called		Type	Rate	Minutes	Amount
Mar 13	5:10 PM	Fanfield, NJ	(906) 555-6896	Direct	Day	2	.52
Mar 19	9:30 PM	Scottsdale, AZ	(602) 555-7145	Direct	Night	6	.76
Mar 27	10:57 AM	Encino, CA	(818) 555-7803	Direct	Eve	10	1.24

•International

Date	Time	Place and Number Called		Type	Rate	Minutes	Amount
Mar 17	8:19 AM	Seoul, Korea	(82) 44-555-3446	Direct	Day	2	2.12
Mar 25	2:00 PM	Warsaw, Poland	(48) 22-555-7863	Direct	Day	6	9.44

2

◆ **Ask your partner about the missing information on the phone bill below.**

◆ **You can use these questions:**

"When did Patrick call _____ ?"

"What time did Patrick make the call to _____ ?"

"How long was the call to _____ ?"

"How much did the call to _____ cost?"

◆ **Write in the missing information and read it back to your partner to check your work.**

Patrick Jensen	Account Number	Statement Date
5231 Oak Dr.	(818) 555-7803	Apr. 14, 2003
Encino, CA		

GTI LONG-DISTANCE CALLS

GTI

•Domestic

Date	Time	Place and Number Called		Type	Rate	Minutes	Amount
Mar 14	6:10 AM	Pelham, NY	(914) 555-9678	Direct	Day		
	3:30 PM	Seattle, WA		Direct	Day	22	
Mar 31		Boulder, CO	(303) 555-3012	Direct			3.04

•International

Date	Time	Place and Number Called		Type	Rate	Minutes	Amount
	8:19 AM	London, GB	(44) 171-555-7000	Direct	Day		5.94
Mar 28		Madrid, Spain		Direct	Night	9	

◆ **What's next?** Look at the time zone map on page 17 of the *Dictionary.* What time was it in each city when Eliza and Patrick made their calls? Who do you think they were calling?

Numbers Puzzle

The Oxford Picture Dictionary, pages 14–15. See page xvii for Teacher's Notes.

Double Crossword

A

◆ **Sit with a partner. (Don't show this paper to your partner!)**

◆ **Take turns giving the clues to complete the puzzle.**

2 down - Roman numeral three

◆ **If your partner needs help, give one letter from the answer on your puzzle.**

The first letter is I.

◆ **When both puzzles are complete, compare your work.**

Clues

2 down — Roman numeral three

3 down — The person after the fifth person in line is the...

4 down — Roman numeral four

6 down — How tall or high something is

8 down — Between seventh and ninth

9 down — Eight plus two

11 down — Four plus three

15 down — Zero plus two

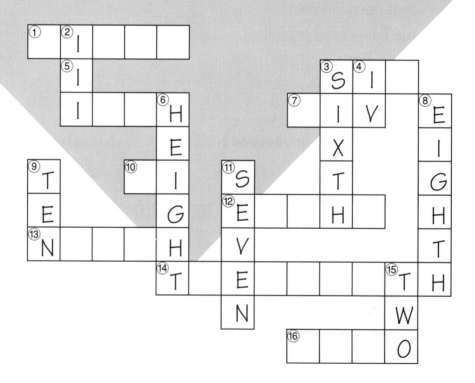

◆ **What's next?** Solve these problems with your partner.

LXI + V =?   C – III =?   (VI + X) – IV =?   (M+XL) – (C+D) =?

Numbers Puzzle

The Oxford Picture Dictionary, pages 14–15. See page xvii for Teacher's Notes.

Double Crossword

B

◆ **Sit with a partner. (Don't show this paper to your partner!)**

◆ **Take turns giving the clues to complete the puzzle.**

  1 across – Between fourth and sixth

◆ **If your partner needs help, give one letter from the answer on your puzzle.**

  The first letter is F.

◆ **When both puzzles are complete, compare your work.**

Clues

1 across — Between fourth and sixth

3 across — Eleven minus five

5 across — 2.54 centimeters equals one of these

7 across — Roman numeral fifty four

10 across — Roman numeral six

12 across — Twelve minus four

13 across — Sixth, seventh, eighth…

14 across — In a race of 20 people, the last person is the…

16 across — 100 minus 100

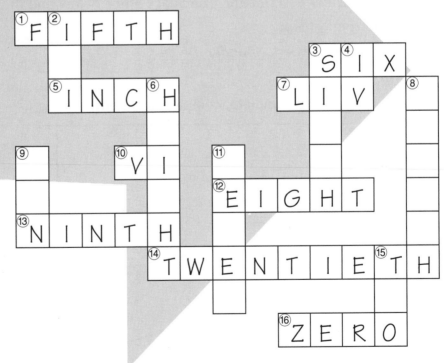

◆ **What's next?** Solve these problems with your partner.

LXI + V =?   C – III =?   (VI + X) – IV =?   (M+XL) – (C+D) =?

What's in her office?

The Oxford Picture Dictionary, pages 2–3, 5, 11, 13. See page xv for Teacher's Notes.

Drawing Dictation

A

1

- ◆ Sit with a partner. (Don't show this paper to your partner!)
- ◆ Describe the counselor's office below.
- ◆ Your partner will draw what you say.
- ◆ Answer your partner's questions.

2

- ◆ Listen to your partner describe the principal's office below and draw what you hear.
- ◆ These questions may help:

  *"Did you say **on** the desk or **under** the desk?"*

  *"**Next to** what?"*

- ◆ When both pictures are complete, compare your work.

- ◆ **What's next?** Describe your classroom to your teacher. Your teacher will draw what you say. Correct your teacher's mistakes.

What's in her office?

The Oxford Picture Dictionary, pages 2–3, 5, 11, 13. See page xv for Teacher's Notes.

Drawing Dictation

1

◆ **Sit with a partner. (Don't show this paper to your partner!)**

◆ **Listen to your partner describe the counselor's office below and draw what you hear.**

◆ **These questions may help:**

   *"Did you say **on** the desk or **under** the desk?"*
   *"**Next to** what?"*

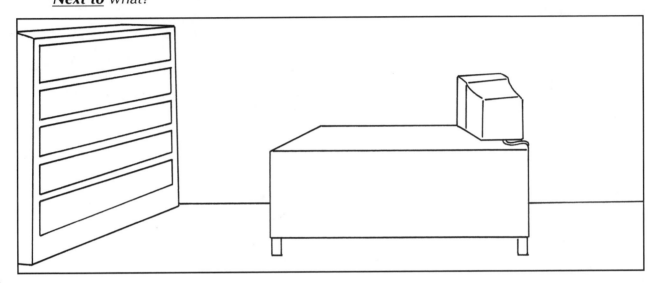

2

◆ **Describe the principal's office below.**

◆ **Your partner will draw what you say.**

◆ **Answer your partner's questions.**

◆ **When both pictures are complete, compare your work.**

◆ **What's next?** Describe your classroom to your teacher. Your teacher will draw what you say. Correct your teacher's mistakes.

School Days

Picture Differences

A

◆ **Sit with a partner and look at each other's papers.**

◆ **There are 10 differences between your pictures.**

◆ **Work with your partner to find the differences.**

◆ **Write the differences you find on the chart below.**

A	B
1. first runner in white	first runner in black
2.	
3.	
4.	
5.	
6.	
7.	
8.	
9.	
10.	

◆ **What's next?** Compare your school to the ones in the pictures. What differences are there?

© 1999 Oxford University Press   Permission granted to reproduce for classroom use.

School Days

The Oxford Picture Dictionary, pages 5, 11. See page xvi for Teacher's Notes.

Picture Differences

B

- ◆ **Sit with a partner and look at each other's papers.**
- ◆ **There are 10 differences between your pictures.**
- ◆ **Work with your partner to find the differences.**

- ◆ **Write the differences you find on the chart below.**

A	B
1. first runner in white	first runner in black
2.	
3.	
4.	
5.	
6.	
7.	
8.	
9.	
10.	

- ◆ **What's next?** Compare your school to the ones in the pictures. What differences are there?

Is it on sale?

The Oxford Picture Dictionary, pages 11–12, 20–21. See page xix for Teacher's Notes.

Role Play

- ◆ **Form groups of 4 people.**
- ◆ **Practice saying all the lines.**
- ◆ **Choose your character and decide what you will say.**
- ◆ **Think of other things your character can say.**
- ◆ **Act out your role play.**

THE SCENE:
A salesclerk in a very busy department store is trying to help three customers find the right color sweater.

THE CHARACTERS:
a salesclerk
a woman
a man
a teenager

THE PROPS:
different colored sweaters (or cut-out pictures of them)

THE SCRIPT:

Who says...	...these lines?
a salesclerk	May I help you?
	I'd like to return* this sweater.
	Excuse me, I was here first.
	I'm looking for a blue sweater.
	That's not my style.
	Can I exchange this for a green sweater?
	We have some great red and green sweaters on sale.
	How much is this sweater?
	It's $15.99 on sale.
	Will that be cash or charge?
	Can I pay by check?

* You can substitute other vocabulary for the underlined words.

- ◆ **What's next?** Plan a garage sale with your class. Bring in and put prices on old books, cassettes, CDs, clothes, toys, and/or kitchen items. Invite one or more classes to shop at your sale. Vote with your classmates on how to spend the money from the sale.

Learn English at Home or at School?

The Oxford Picture Dictionary, pages 5–7. See page xx for Teacher's Notes.

Take a Stand

- **Think about the reasons to learn English at home or to learn it at school.**
- **Read each statement on the list.**
- **If the statement shows that <u>learning at home</u> is a good idea, make a ✓ in that column.**
- **If the statement shows that <u>learning in school</u> is a good idea, make a ✓ in that column.**
- **For K and L, think of two more statements to add to this list.**

STATEMENTS	Home	School
A. Some students live far away from a school.		
B. You can study at any time of the night or day.		
C. There are programs on TV that teach English.		
D. You can use the gym, field, and library at school.		
E. Teachers have many different ways of teaching English.		
F. Many schools have counselors that will help students.		
G. You can buy textbooks and cassettes to use at home.		
H. Many classes have more than 30 students.		
I. You have to talk to people in English to learn English well.		
J. Most English classes at public schools in the U.S. are free.		
K.		
L.		

- **Sit with a partner and compare papers.**
- **Write your and your partner's ideas.**

I think it is better to learn English _____ *because* _____

_____.

My partner thinks it is better to learn English _____ *because* _____

_____.

- **What's next?** Take a stand. Your teacher will tell you where to stand if you support learning English at home and where to stand if you support learning English at school.

Everyday Language Board.

Draw
a clock and describe what you've drawn.

Name
three kinds of numbers.

Pick a weather card. Say 3 things about it.

Answer:
Do you prefer cool weather or warm weather? Why?

In 15 seconds...
name 5 different colors.

Act out
a classroom verb for your group. (The group has to guess what it is!)

To begin...
- Put your markers on start.
- Take turns flipping a coin to move your marker around the board.

moves one space

moves two spaces

- Follow the directions on the squares.
- Ask your group for help when you don't know the answer.

Finish

Name something
you open everyday.

Pick a weather card.

Spell it.

Start

Game

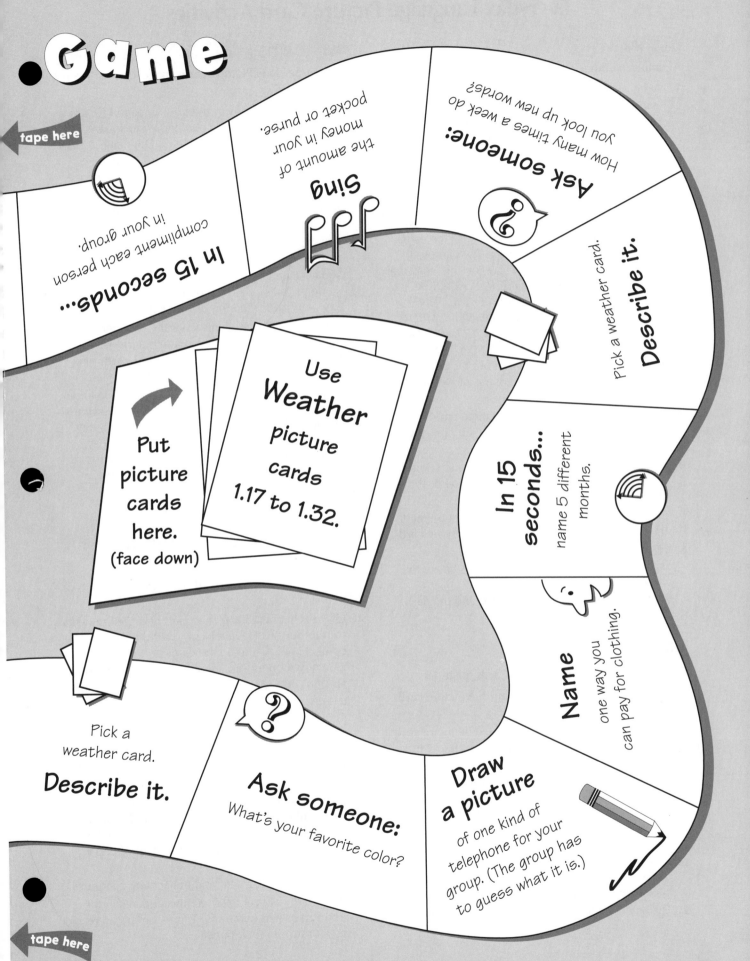

tape here

In 15 seconds...
compliment each person in your group.

Sing
the amount of money in your pocket or purse.

Ask someone:
How many times a week do you look up new words?

Pick a weather card.
Describe it.

Use
Weather
picture
cards
1.17 to 1.32.

Put
picture
cards
here.
(face down)

In 15 seconds...
name 5 different months.

Name
one way you can pay for clothing.

Pick a
weather card.
Describe it.

Ask someone:
What's your favorite color?

Draw a picture
of one kind of telephone for your group. (The group has to guess what it is.)

tape here

Everyday Language Picture Card Activities

A–Z (Pairs)

Alphabet/Number Cards, page 17

1. Write a dash, a period, an apostrophe, a question mark, and a comma on the five blank squares of the alphabet/number card page. Duplicate a class set of the page and have students cut the cards apart. (Have students separate the alphabet cards into one pile, the number cards into another, and the dash/period/apostrophe/question mark/comma cards into a third.)

2. Call out different words, spelling them letter by letter and have individual students use the cards to make the word on their desk. You can use the following words from pages 2–4 (or any word that does not repeat a letter): *CHAIR, SEAT, DESK, OPEN, CLOSE, RAISE, POINT, PENCIL, PEN, MARKER, BINDER, ERASER, RULER, NUMBERS, PICTURE, MAP, GLOBE, CLOCK, COMPUTER, FIRST NAME, PHONE, MONTH, DATE, YEAR, BIRTH, PRINT, SIGN.* (You can use the period or apostrophe to spell out other kinds of words, e.g. *MRS. KING, CAN'T,* etc.

3. Once you have dictated two or three words, see if students can guess the word after you have given them only two or three letters.

4. Pair students and have partners face each other, with only one partner (A) facing the board. Write six of the words above, on the board.

5. Direct all the A's to dictate one word at a time to the B partners. B's make the words with the cards.

6. Have students change places. Write six new words on the board and have the B's dictate to the A's.
   Variation: Using the number cards and the dash, dictate phone numbers.

PICK A PAIR (Pairs)

Classroom/Prepositions Picture Cards, page 18

1. Pair students and give each pair one picture card page.

2. Have the pair cut up the cards, shuffle them, and place them face down in four rows of four cards.

3. Have partners take turns turning over two cards at a time, trying to get both a preposition and a classroom object card. When one of each card is turned over, for example, *pencil* and *on,* the student keeps the cards if she can make a sentence: *The pencil's on the box.* If the student can't say the sentence correctly, or two of the same kind of cards are turned over, the student turns the cards back over and the next student goes.

4. The activity ends when all the cards are gone.

TWIN GRIDS (Pairs)

Weather/Seasons Picture Cards, page 19
Grid, page 197

1. Duplicate one copy of the grid on page 197 and write in 16 city names, one name per square. (Los Angeles, New York, Dallas, etc.) Duplicate a class set of this grid and the picture card page. Give each student one grid and one picture card page.

2. Have students cut apart their picture cards and place them spread out and face up, on their desks next to the grid.

3. Tell students, *It's raining in New York.* Direct students to place the picture of rain on the grid square with New York's name in it. Encourage students to ask clarification questions. *Did you say New York? Raining or snowing?*

4. Continue telling students what the weather is in various cities until all the weather cards are used up. Have students compare their grids with one another as you clarify any discrepancies.

5. Next, pair students. Give each pair a manila folder to use as a screen between the partners. Have the sender tell the receiver the weather in each city. (Students do not have to copy your sentences.) Both partners place their pictures on the grids. When the grids are complete, senders and receivers compare their grids.

6. Have senders and receivers switch roles.

NOW AND THEN CHARADES (Groups)

Classroom Verbs Picture Cards, page 20

1. Duplicate one picture card page for each group of 4–5 students.

2. Give each group one picture card page. Tell students to number off. Have #1 cut apart the picture cards. Have #2 shuffle the cards and place them face down on a desk. Identify #4 as the recorder.

3. For the first round, Student #1 picks a card from the deck, asks *What am I doing?,* and pantomimes the action until the group can name it. Once the group names the action, for example, *You're writing,* student #1 sits down.

4. The recorder then asks the group, *What did Carlos do?* Group members reach consensus on the correct way to put the sentence in the past, using the **Verb Guide** on pages 170–172 in the *Dictionary* to check the correct past tense form. The recorder writes the group's response on a sheet of paper e.g., *Carlos wrote.*

5. Student #2 picks a card and the activity continues.

6. The activity is over when all the students in the group have had two turns. The recorder can read from or turn in their papers.

Alphabet/Number Cards

G	N	U	1	8	
F	M	T	0	7	
E	L	S	Z	6	
D	K	R	Y	5	
C	J	Q	X	4	
B	I	P	W	3	10
A	H	O	V	2	9

Picture Cards: Classroom/Prepositions

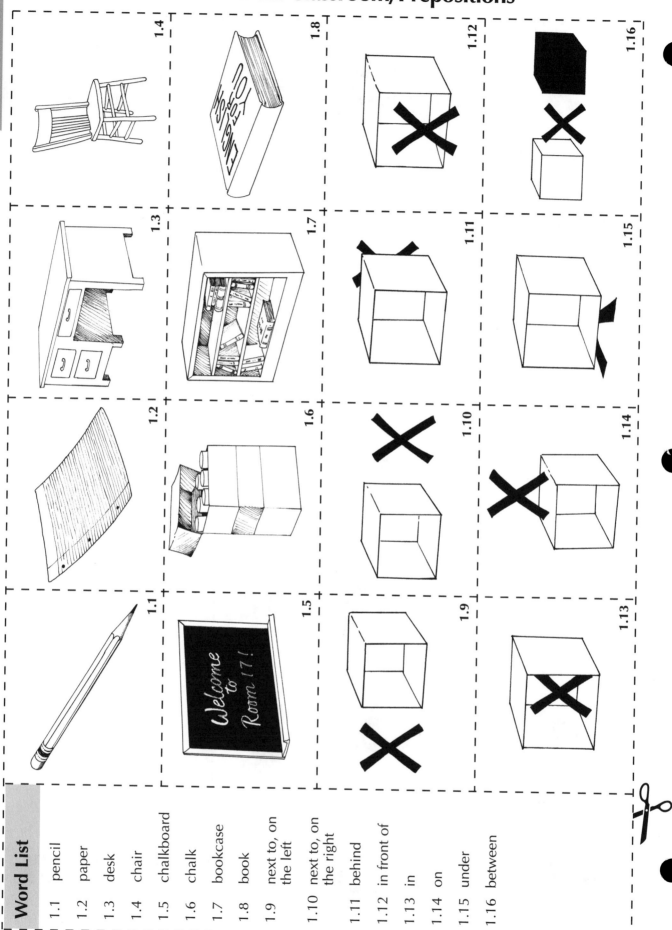

Word List		
1.1	pencil	
1.2	paper	
1.3	desk	
1.4	chair	
1.5	chalkboard	
1.6	chalk	
1.7	bookcase	
1.8	book	
1.9	next to, on the left	
1.10	next to, on the right	
1.11	behind	
1.12	in front of	
1.13	in	
1.14	on	
1.15	under	
1.16	between	

Picture Cards: Weather/Seasons

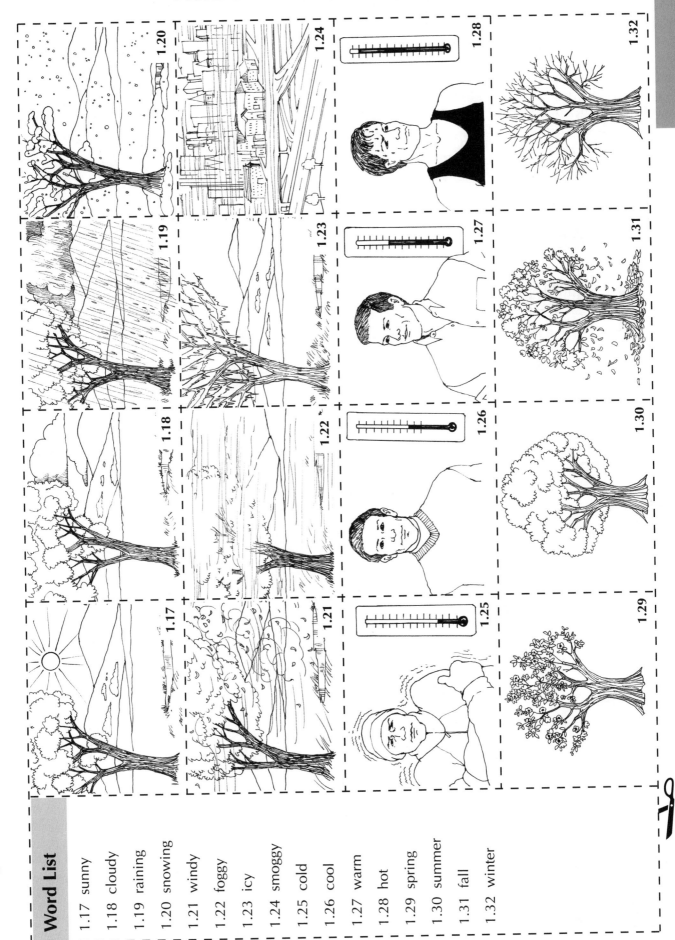

Picture Cards: Classroom Verbs

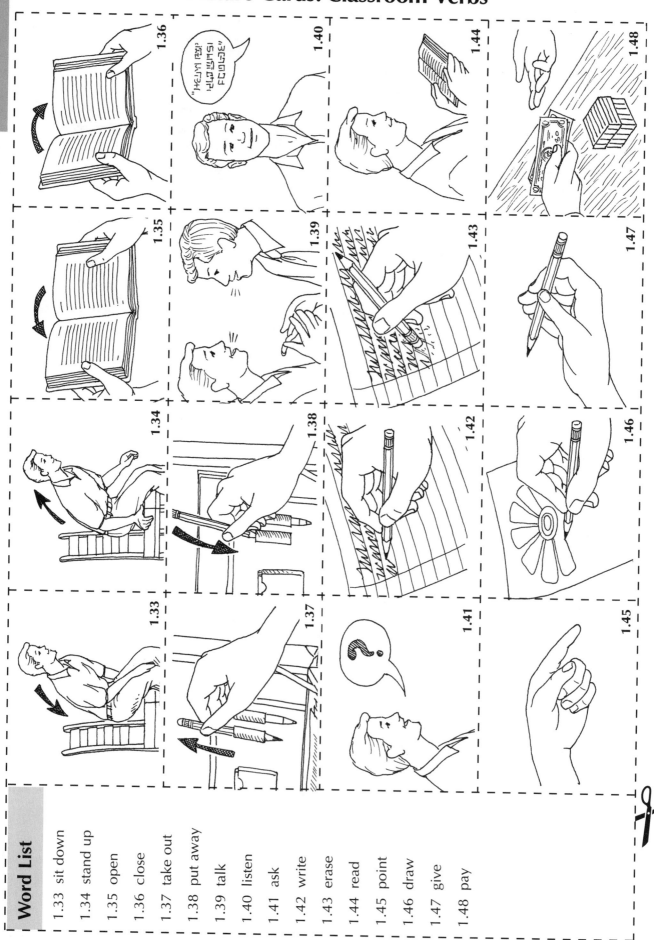

© 1999 Oxford University Press   Permission granted to reproduce for classroom use.

2. People

What kind of people are at the party?

The Oxford Picture Dictionary, page 22. See page xii for Teacher's Notes.

◆ Form groups of 4 people.

◆ Each person in the group takes turns labeling the people on this paper.

◆ After all the people are labeled, look in the *Dictionary* to check your group's work.

◆ **What's next?** Draw a picture of a child, a teenager, or an adult that you know. Write a description of your picture. You can use the example below to help you. Remember to use different words for your descriptions. *This is a picture of my niece, Ida. She's six years old. She's average weight and average height for her age. Her hair is red and curly. She's a cute little girl.* Share your picture with the class.

We are an interesting class!

The Oxford Picture Dictionary, pages 28–29. See page xiii for Teacher's Notes.

Mixer

- ◆ **Write the missing words on the lines.**
- ◆ **Your teacher will tell you the dates to write for each question.**
- ◆ **Walk around the room. Ask and answer the questions.**
- ◆ **Write a different name in each box.**

1. Were you _____ born _____ before _____ 1975 _____ ?

Yes	No

2. Did you _____ to drive after _____ ?

Yes	No

3. Did you _____ a job before _____ ?

Yes	No

4. Did you _____ in _____ ?

Yes	No

5. Did you _____ before _____ ?

Yes	No

6. Did you _____ school after _____ ?

Yes	No

7. Did you _____ before _____ ?

Yes	No

- ◆ **What's next?** Discuss your answers with your class.

What a day!

The Oxford Picture Dictionary, pages 24–25. 26–27. See page xvi for Teacher's Notes.

◆ **Sit with a partner and look at each other's papers.**

◆ **There are 10 differences between your pictures.**

◆ **Work with your partner to find the differences.**

◆ **Write the differences you find on the chart below.**

A	B
1. son is getting up	son is not getting up
2.	
3.	
4.	
5.	
6.	
7.	
8.	
9.	
10.	

◆ **What's next?** Talk about your daily routine with your partner. What's the same? What's different?

What a day!

The Oxford Picture Dictionary, pages 24–25. 26–27. See page xvi for Teacher's Notes.

Picture Differences

B

- ◆ **Sit with a partner and look at each other's papers.**
- ◆ **There are 10 differences between your pictures.**
- ◆ **Work with your partner to find the differences.**

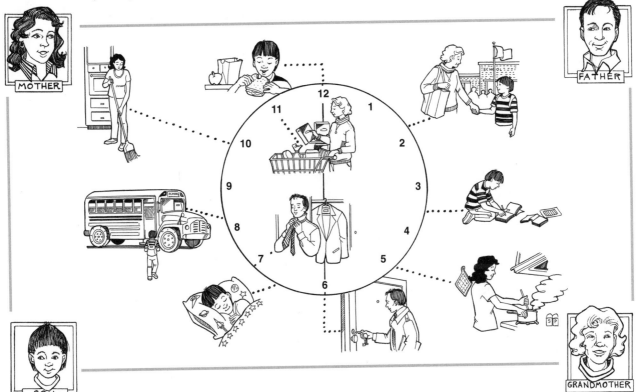

- ◆ **Write the differences you find on the chart below.**

A	B
1. son is getting up	son is not getting up
2.	
3.	
4.	
5.	
6.	
7.	
8.	
9.	
10.	

- ◆ **What's next?** Talk about your daily routine with your partner. What's the same? What's different?

Graduation Puzzle

The Oxford Picture Dictionary, pages 32–33. See page xvii for Teacher's Notes.

Double Crossword

A

◆ **Sit with a partner. (Don't show this paper to your partner!)**

◆ **Take turns giving the clues to complete the puzzle.**

  2 across — This is what graduates wear over their clothes

◆ **If your partner needs help, give one letter from the answer on your puzzle.**

  The first letter is G.

◆ **When both puzzles are complete, compare your work.**

Clues

2 across — This is what graduates wear over their clothes

3 across — This is the paper graduates get

4 across — This is what graduates wear on their heads

8 across — The graduate with the best grades is the...

9 across — Page 32 shows a graduation...

10 across — This is what some people do when they watch a graduation

11 across — A speaker makes this

13 across — When you hear something funny you do this

◆ **What's next?** Work with a partner to come up with two more clues for other words on pages 32 and 33 in the *Dictionary*. See if the class can guess the words from your clues.

Graduation Puzzle

The Oxford Picture Dictionary, pages 32–33. See page xvii for Teacher's Notes.　　**Double Crossword**

B

- ◆ **Sit with a partner. (Don't show this paper to your partner!)**
- ◆ **Take turns giving the clues to complete the puzzle.**

    1 down — This decoration sometimes has the word "Congratulations" on it

- ◆ **If your partner needs help, give one letter from the answer on your puzzle.**

    The first letter is B.

- ◆ **When both puzzles are complete, compare your work.**

Clues

1 down — This decoration sometimes has the word "Congratulations" on it

2 down — A person who comes to a party is a…

3 down — Another word for disc jockey

5 down — A person who prepares food for parties is a…

6 down — A person who takes pictures professionally is a…

7 down — People can have this to celebrate a birthday or graduation

9 down — Another word for "applaud"

12 down — Friends do this when they see each other at a party

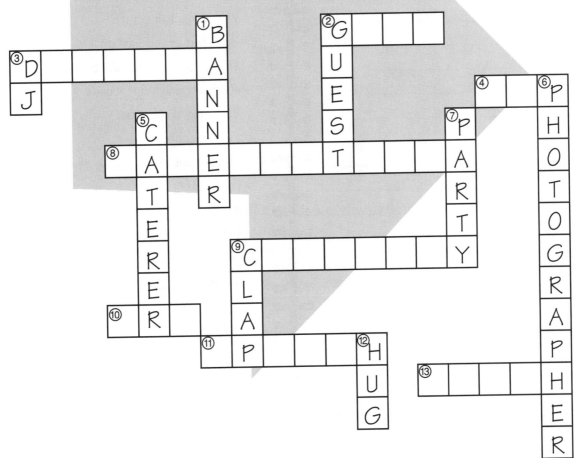

- ◆ **What's next?**　Work with a partner to come up with two more clues for other words on pages 32 and 33 in the *Dictionary*. See if the class can guess the words from your clues.

Please, don't cut it too short!

Role Play

- ◆ **Form groups of 4 people.**
- ◆ **Practice saying all the lines.**
- ◆ **Choose your character and decide what you will say.**
- ◆ **Think of other things your character can say.**
- ◆ **Act out your role play.**

THE PROPS:
an appointment book
one or two mirrors
a comb and a brush
pictures of hairstyles
from magazines

THE CHARACTERS:
a receptionist
one or two customers
a hair stylist

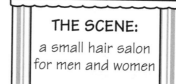

THE SCENE:
a small hair salon
for men and women

THE SCRIPT:

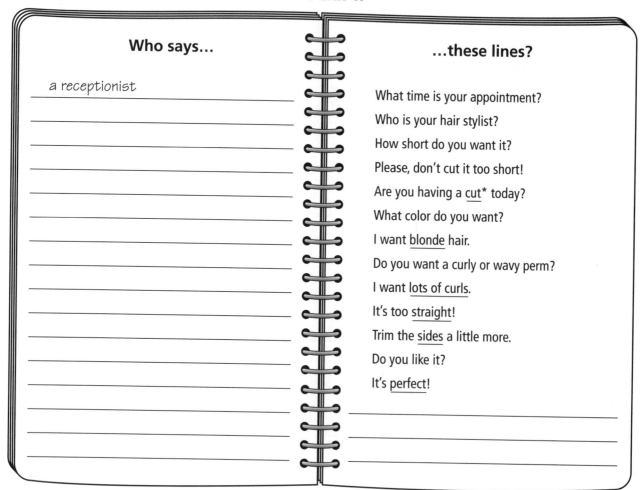

Who says...	...these lines?
a receptionist	What time is your appointment?
	Who is your hair stylist?
	How short do you want it?
	Please, don't cut it too short!
	Are you having a <u>cut</u>* today?
	What color do you want?
	I want <u>blonde</u> hair.
	Do you want a curly or wavy perm?
	I want <u>lots of curls</u>.
	It's too <u>straight</u>!
	Trim the <u>sides</u> a little more.
	Do you like it?
	It's <u>perfect</u>!

* You can substitute other vocabulary for the underlined words.

- ◆ **What's next?** Talk about your experiences with hair stylists.

Which is Better — Small or Large Families?

The Oxford Picture Dictionary, pages 24–25. See page xx for Teacher's Notes.

Take a Stand

- ◆ **Think about the reasons to have a small or large family.**
- ◆ **Read each statement on the list.**
- ◆ **If the statement shows that a <u>small family</u> is a good idea, make a ✓ in that column.**
- ◆ **If the statement shows that a <u>large family</u> is a good idea, make a ✓ in that column.**
- ◆ **For K and L, think of two more statements to add to this list.**

STATEMENTS		
A. Older children can baby-sit.		
B. Food, clothing and medicine are expensive.		
C. Children can help their parents at work.		
D. Children in large families sometimes share bedrooms.		
E. Older children show a good example for their brothers and sisters.		
F. Relatives help each other with family problems.		
G. Travel is easier and cheaper for small families.		
H. When parents get old, their children can take care of them.		
I. Grandparents are very proud of their grandchildren.		
J. Nobody understands you as well as your family.		
K.		
L.		

- ◆ **Sit with a partner and compare papers.**
- ◆ **Write your and your partner's ideas.**

I think _____ *families are better because* _____

_____.

My partner thinks _____ *families are better because* _____

_____.

- ◆ **What's next?** Take a stand. Your teacher will tell you where to stand if you support large families and where to stand if you support small families.

People Board

tape here

Draw
a famous person. Describe him or her.

Name
an important personal paper that you have.

Pick a feelings card. Say 3 things about it.

Answer:
What do you need to make a great party?

In 15 seconds...
name 5 things you do to your hair.

Act out
a daily routine for your group. (The group has to guess what it is!)

To begin...
- Put your markers on start.
- Take turns flipping a coin to move your marker around the board.

moves one space

moves two spaces

- Follow the directions on the squares.
- Ask your group for help when you don't know the answer.

Finish

Start

Pick a feelings card.
Spell it.

Name something
at a graduation ceremony.

tape here

Game

tape here

In 15 seconds...
name 5 people in your family.

Sing
a song about your daily routine.

Ask someone:
What's the best age to get married? Why?

Pick a feelings card.
Describe it.

Put picture cards here.
(face down)

Use Feelings picture cards 2.1 to 2.16.

In 15 seconds...
name 5 words to describe people.

Name
something you do before school.

Pick a feelings card.
Describe it.

Ask someone:
What important thing happened to you this year?

Draw a picture
of someone in your class. (The group has to guess who it is.)

tape here

People Picture Card Activities

NOW AND THEN CHARADES (Groups)

Feelings Picture Cards, page 33

1. Duplicate one picture card page for each group of 4-5 students.

2. Group students and give each group one picture card page. Tell students to number off. Have #1 cut apart the picture cards. Have #2 shuffle the cards and place them face down on a desk. Identify #4 as the recorder.

3. For the first round, Student #1 picks a card from the deck, asks *How do I feel?*, and pantomimes the action until the group can name it. Once the group names the action, for example, *You feel hungry.*, student #1 sits down.

4. The recorder then asks the group, *How did Carlos feel?* Group members reach consensus on the correct way to write the sentence, using the *Dictionary*, pages 31-32 to check the correct spelling. The recorder writes the group's response on a sheet of paper. *Carlos felt hungry.*

5. Student #2 picks a card and the activity continues.

6. The activity is over when all the students in the group have had two turns. Recorders can read from or turn in their papers.

MIXER (Whole Class)

Life Events Picture Cards, page 34

1. Duplicate enough copies of the picture card page so that each student can have one card.

2. Give half of the students a life event (verb) card. These students are celebrating an important life event. Give the other half a document (noun) card. These students are clerks in the Department of Records. Have all the students holding life events cards go to one side of the room and all the clerks holding document cards go to the other.

3. Have students go up to the clerks to get the correct document.

    I just had a baby. I need to get an official document. Can you help me?

    -Yes. Here's the birth certificate. OR

    -I'm sorry. I don't have what you need. I only have driver's licenses.

4. The activity ends when everyone finds a correct match.

PICK A PAIR (Pairs)

Age/Physical Description Picture Cards, page 35

1. Duplicate half a class set of the picture cards page.

2. Pair students and give each pair one picture card page.

3. Have the pair cut up the cards, shuffle them, and place them face down in four rows of four cards.

4. Have partners take turns turning over two cards at a time, trying to match pictures depicting opposite characteristics of the same people. When the cards match, for example, *young woman/elderly woman*, the student keeps the cards if she can make a sentence: *In this picture, Ana is a young woman, but in the other picture, she's old.* If the student can't say a sentence, or the cards don't match (*young woman/thin man*) the student turns the cards back over and the next student goes.

5. The activity ends when all the cards are gone.

TWIN GRIDS (Pairs)

Daily Routines Picture Cards, page 36
Grid, page 197

1. Duplicate one copy of the grid on page 197 and mark a time indicating A.M. or P.M. for each square. Give each student one grid and one picture card page.

2. Have students cut apart their picture cards and place them spread out and face up, on their desks next to the grid.

3. Tell students that "Susan" (substitute any name, fictitious or real) wakes up at 7:00 A.M. Direct students to place the picture showing "wake up" on the 7 A.M. grid square. Encourage students to ask clarification questions. *Did you say wake up? 7:00 a.m. or p.m.?*

4. Continue telling students what Susan does at different times until all the grid squares are filled. Have students compare their grids with one another as you clarify any discrepancies.

5. Next, pair students. Give each pair a manila folder to use as a screen between the partners. Have sender tell the receiver Susan's schedule. (Students do not have to copy your sentences.) Both partners place their pictures on the grids. When the grids are complete, senders and receivers compare their grids.

6. Have the senders and the receivers switch roles.

Picture Cards: Feelings

Word List

2.1	hungry
2.2	sleepy
2.3	calm
2.4	nervous
2.5	happy
2.6	sad
2.7	angry
2.8	scared
2.9	surprised
2.10	tired
2.11	embarrassed
2.12	thirsty
2.13	sick
2.14	confused
2.15	bored
2.16	frustrated

Picture Cards: Life Events

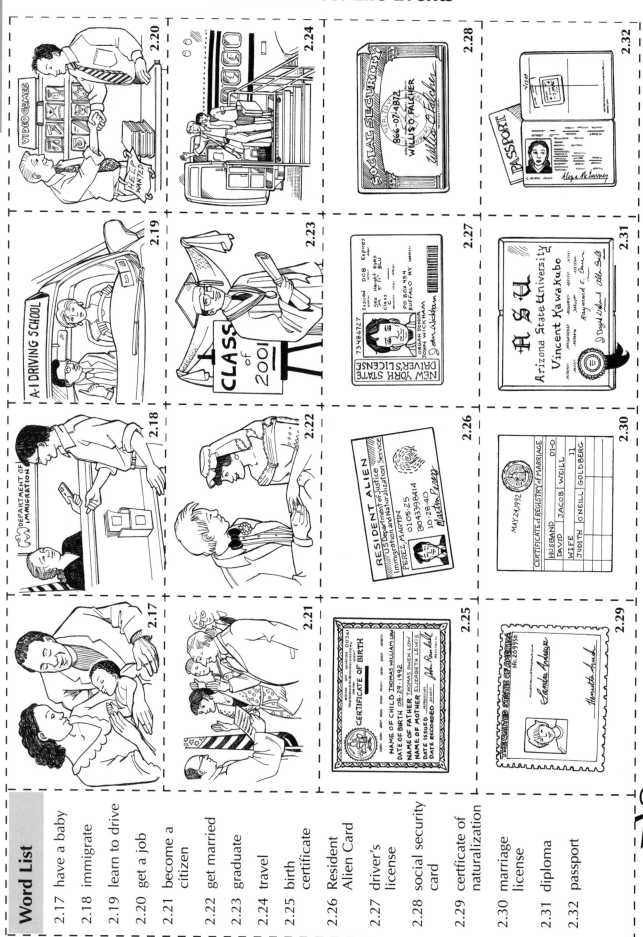

2.20

2.24

2.28

2.32

2.19

2.23

2.27

2.31

2.18

2.22

2.26

2.30

2.17

2.21

2.25

2.29

Word List

2.17 have a baby

2.18 immigrate

2.19 learn to drive

2.20 get a job

2.21 become a citizen

2.22 get married

2.23 graduate

2.24 travel

2.25 birth certificate

2.26 Resident Alien Card

2.27 driver's license

2.28 social security card

2.29 certificate of naturalization

2.30 marriage license

2.31 diploma

2.32 passport

Picture Cards: Age/Physical Description

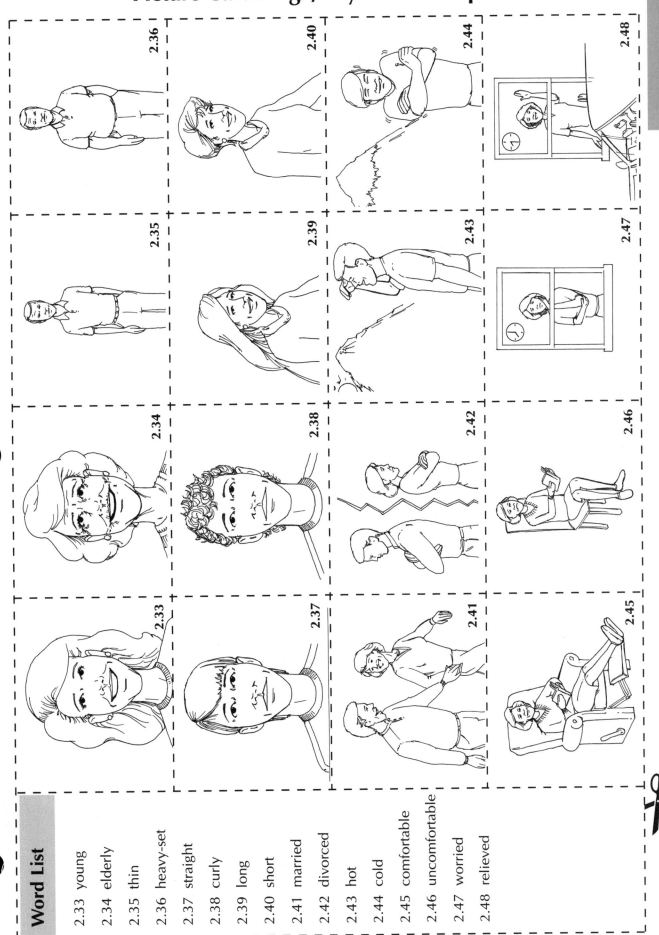

2.36

2.35

2.34

2.33

2.40

2.39

2.38

2.37

2.44

2.43

2.42

2.41

2.48

2.47

2.46

2.45

Word List

2.33 young
2.34 elderly
2.35 thin
2.36 heavy-set
2.37 straight
2.38 curly
2.39 long
2.40 short
2.41 married
2.42 divorced
2.43 hot
2.44 cold
2.45 comfortable
2.46 uncomfortable
2.47 worried
2.48 relieved

Picture Cards: Daily Routines

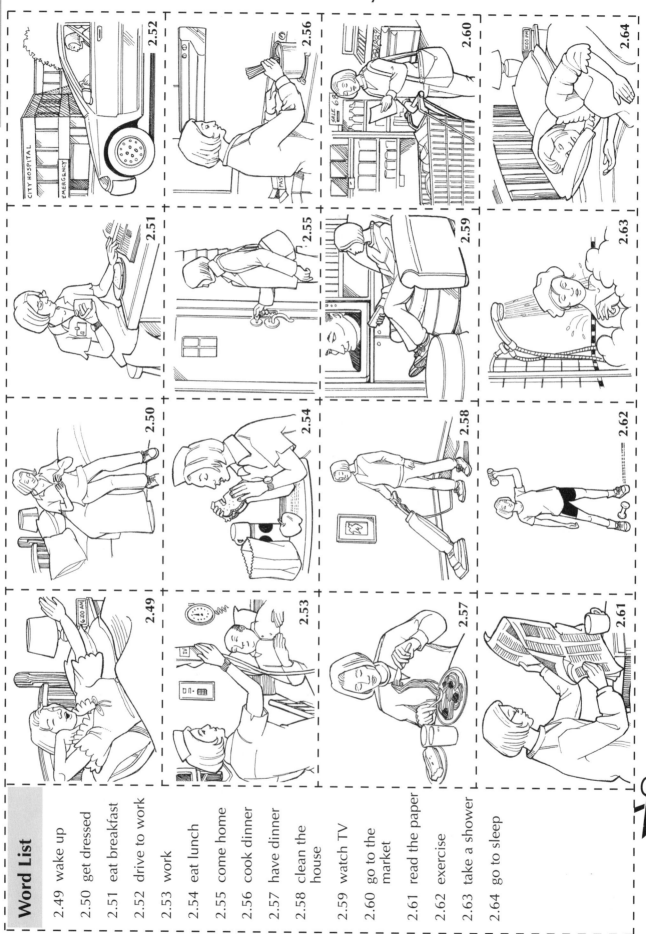

2.49 wake up
2.50 get dressed
2.51 eat breakfast
2.52 drive to work
2.53 work
2.54 eat lunch
2.55 come home
2.56 cook dinner
2.57 have dinner
2.58 clean the house
2.59 watch TV
2.60 go to the market
2.61 read the paper
2.62 exercise
2.63 take a shower
2.64 go to sleep

3. Housing

Page(s)		Places to Live (34)	Finding a Home (35)	Apartments (36–37)	A House (38)	A Yard (39)	A Kitchen (40)	A Dining Area (41)	A Living Room (42)	A Bathroom (43)	A Bedroom (44)	A Children's Bedroom (45)	Housework (46)	Cleaning Supplies (47)	Household Problems and Repairs (48–49)
38	**A Yard Sale!** (Round Table Label)					◆		◆		◆	◆				
39	**There's no place like home!** (Mixer)	◆													
40–41	**The Perfect Kitchen!** (Drawing Dictation)						◆								
42–43	**Home and Yard** (Double Crossword)				◆	◆									
44	**You'll love this apartment!** (Role Play)			◆											
45	**An Apartment or a House?** (Take a Stand)			◆	◆	◆									
46–47	**Housing Board Game** (Board Game)	◆	◆	◆	◆	◆	◆	◆	◆	◆	◆	◆	◆	◆	◆
48–52	**Picture Card Activities and Picture Cards**					◆	◆	◆	◆				◆	◆	◆

A Yard Sale!

The Oxford Picture Dictionary, pages 39, 42, 44–45. See page xii for Teacher's Notes.

- ◆ **Form groups of 4 people.**
- ◆ **Each person in the group takes turns labeling the items on this paper.**
- ◆ **After all the pictures have labels, look in the *Dictionary* to check your group's work.**

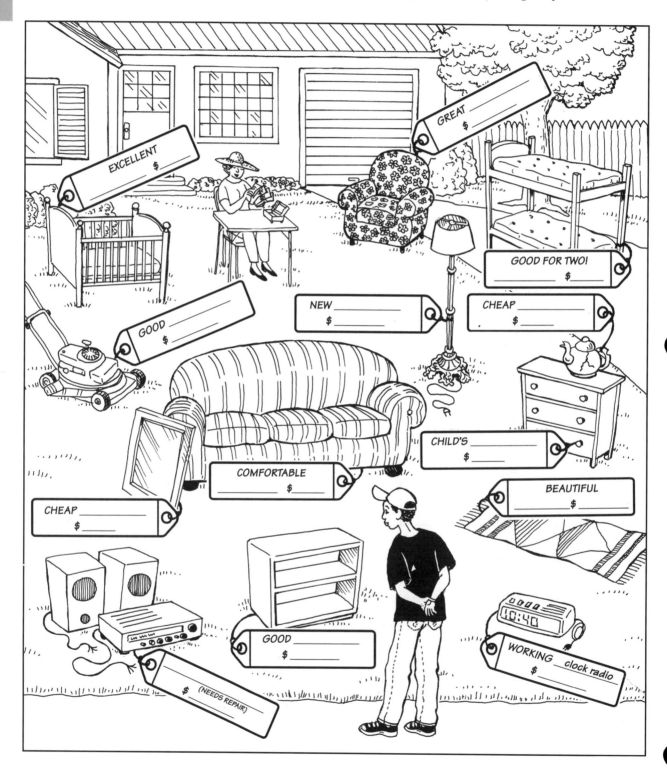

- ◆ **What's next?** Decide on a price for each item. Take turns being the buyer and seller at a garage sale.

There's no place like home!

The Oxford Picture Dictionary, page 34. See page xiii for Teacher's Notes.

- ◆ **Write the missing letters for each word.**
- ◆ **Walk around the room. Ask and answer the questions.**
- ◆ **Write a different name in each box.**

Have you ever lived on a farm?

1. Have you ever lived on a <u>f a r m</u> ?

Yes	No

2. Have you ever lived in a <u>h _ _ _ _ _</u> ?

Yes	No

3. Have you ever lived in a small <u>t _ _ _ _</u> ?

Yes	No

4. Have you ever lived in a big <u>c _ _ _ _</u> ?

Yes	No

5. Have you ever lived on a <u>r _ _ _ _ _</u> ?

Yes	No

6. Have you ever lived in a <u>m _ _ _ _ _ _</u> <u>h _ _ _ _</u> ?

Yes	No

7. Have you ever lived in the <u>c _ _ _ _ _ _ _</u> ?

Yes	No

- ◆ **What's next?** Discuss your answers with your class.

The Perfect Kitchen!

The Oxford Picture Dictionary, page 40. See page xv for Teacher's Notes.

A

❶

- ◆ Sit with a partner. (Don't show this paper to your partner!)
- ◆ Describe Rina's kitchen.
- ◆ Your partner will draw what you say.
- ◆ Answer your partner's questions.

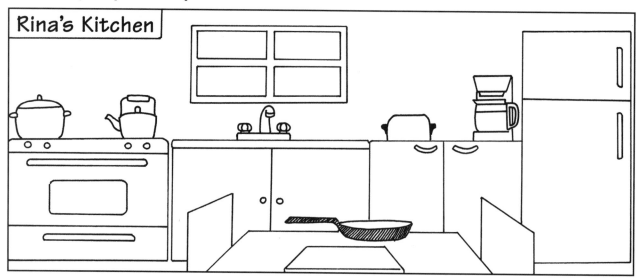

Rina's Kitchen

❷

- ◆ Listen to your partner describe Sol's kitchen and draw what you hear.
- ◆ These questions may help:

  *"Did you say **stove**?" "Is that <u>on the **right** or on the **left**</u>?"*

- ◆ When both pictures are complete, compare your work.

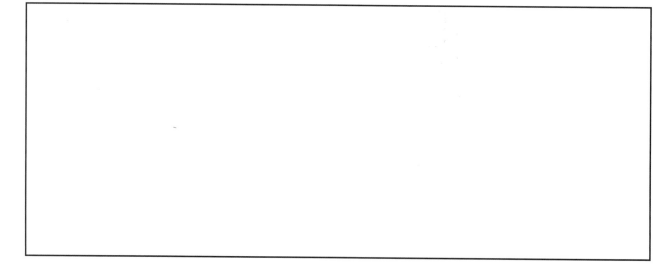

- ◆ **What's next?** Describe a kitchen to your teacher. Your teacher will draw what you say. Correct your teacher's mistakes.

40 Unit Three

© 1999 Oxford University Press   Permission granted to reproduce for classroom use.

The Perfect Kitchen!

The Oxford Picture Dictionary, page 40. See page xv for Teacher's Notes.

- ◆ **Sit with a partner. (Don't show this paper to your partner!)**
- ◆ **Listen to your partner describe Rina's kitchen and draw what you hear.**
- ◆ **These questions may help:**

  *"Did you say **stove**?" "Is that <u>on the **right**</u> or on the **left**?"*

- ◆ **When both pictures are complete, compare your work.**

- ◆ **Describe Sol's kitchen.**
- ◆ **Your partner will draw what you say.**
- ◆ **Answer your partner's questions.**

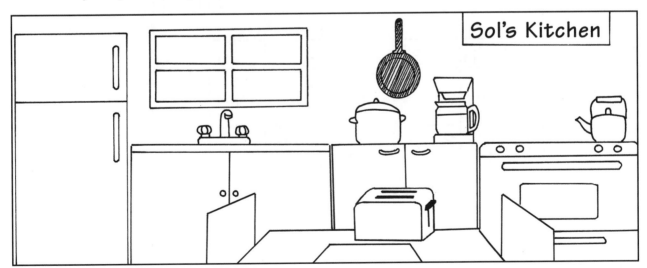

Sol's Kitchen

- ◆ **What's next?** Describe a kitchen to your teacher. Your teacher will draw what you say. Correct your teacher's mistakes.

Home and Yard

Double Crossword

A

- ◆ **Sit with a partner. (Don't show this paper to your partner!)**
- ◆ **Take turns giving the clues to complete the puzzle.**

  2 across — You open this to enter the house

- ◆ **If your partner needs help, give one letter from the answer on your puzzle.**

  The second letter is O.

- ◆ **When both puzzles are complete, compare your work.**

Clues

2 across — You open this to enter the house

5 across — Smoke comes out of here

6 across — This is on top of the house

8 across — You can sleep outside in this

9 across — You cook here

10 across — You can carry a lot of things in this

13 across — You walk up these into the house

15 across — You get mail here

16 across — You park your car here

- ◆ **What's next?** Talk with your partner. Are houses in the U.S. the same as houses in your country? What's different?

Home and Yard

The Oxford Picture Dictionary, pages 38–39. See page xvii for Teacher's Notes.

Double Crossword

B

- ◆ **Sit with a partner. (Don't show this paper to your partner!)**
- ◆ **Take turns giving the clues to complete the puzzle.**

    1 down — You can eat outside here

- ◆ **If your partner needs help, give one letter from the answer on your puzzle.**

    The second letter is A.

- ◆ **When both puzzles are complete, compare your work.**

Clues

1 down — You can eat outside here

2 down — This is a wooden patio in the backyard

3 down — You sleep in this room

4 down — This is the area behind the house

6 down — You can sweep leaves with this

7 down — This goes all around the yard

11 down — This is long and thin and carries water

12 down — You can see through this

14 down — This is in the garden and comes in many color

① P
A
T
I
O

② D
E
C
K

③ B
E
D
R
O
O
M

④ B
A
C
K
Y
A
R
D

⑤ C

⑥ R
A
K
E

⑦ F
E
N
C
E

⑧

⑨ K

⑩ ⑪ H
O
U
S
E

⑫ W
I
N
D
O
W

⑬

⑭ F
L
O
W
E
R

⑮

⑯

- ◆ **What's next?** Talk with your partner. Are houses in the U.S. the same as houses in your country? What's different?

You'll love this apartment!

The Oxford Picture Dictionary, pages 36–37. See page xix for Teacher's Notes.

- ◆ **Form groups of 3–4 people.**
- ◆ **Practice saying all the lines.**
- ◆ **Choose your character and decide what you will say.**
- ◆ **Think of other things your character can say.**
- ◆ **Act out your role play.**

THE SCENE:
Two people looking for an apartment are sitting in the manager's office.

THE CHARACTERS:
a landlord
two or three possible renters
(They can be husband and wife, two friends, etc.)

THE PROPS:
some papers
(a lease and a list of apartment rules)

THE SCRIPT:

Who says...	...these lines?
renter #1	How much is the rent?
	The rent is $750* a month.
	How big is the apartment?
	Is it furnished or unfurnished?
	It is furnished.
	Does it have air conditioning or a swimming pool?
	It has air conditioning but no pool.
	Who pays for utilities?
	Don't worry about it. You don't have to pay!
	Can we have pets?
	Sorry, you can't have pets.
	Are the neighbors noisy?
	The neighbors are noisy but wonderful.

*You can substitute other vocabulary for the underlined words.

- ◆ **What's next?** Tell what happened to you when you rented an apartment.

An Apartment or a House?

The Oxford Picture Dictionary, pages 36–39. See page xx for Teacher's Notes.

- ◆ **Think about the reasons to live in an apartment or a house.**
- ◆ **Read each statement on the list.**
- ◆ **If the statement shows that <u>living in an apartment</u> is a good idea, make a ✔ in that column.**
- ◆ **If the statement shows that <u>living in a house</u> is a good idea, make a ✔ in that column.**
- ◆ **For K and L, think of two more statements to add to this list.**

STATEMENTS	🏢	🏠
A. People live near each other in an apartment.		
B. An apartment usually rents for between $400–$900 a month.		
C. You can usually change things in a house you own.		
D. In an apartment the landlord has to fix broken things.		
E. In a house you pay for all the electricity and water bills.		
F. You can move out of an apartment with one month's notice.		
G. You are responsible for the yard and garden in a house.		
H. Neighbors usually can't hear you in a house.		
I. An apartment usually comes with a stove.		
J. Many houses have gardens and yards.		
K.		
L.		

- ◆ **Sit with a partner and compare papers.**
- ◆ **Write your and your partner's ideas.**

Right now I think it is better to live in a(n) _____ *because*

_____.

Right now my partner thinks it is better to live in a(n) _____

because _____.

- ◆ **What's next?** Take a stand. Your teacher will tell you where to stand if you support living in an apartment and where to stand if you support living in a house. When you finish, write four sentences describing your perfect house or apartment.

Housing Board

Draw
something you
see on the
outside of a house.
(The group has to
guess what it is!)

Name
one thing you
do after you rent
an apartment.

**Pick a
housing card.**
Say 3 things
about it.

Answer:
Do you like to repair
things yourself or do
you call a repair
person? Why?

**In 15
seconds...**
name 3 different people
who can repair a house.

Act out
a gardening verb
for your group.
(The group has to
guess it!)

To begin...

- Put your markers on start.
- Take turns flipping a coin to move your marker around the board.

moves one space

moves two spaces

- Follow the directions on the squares.
- Ask your group for help when you don't know the answer.

Finish

Start

**Pick a
housing
card.
Spell it.**

Name
something you
can do in
the garden.

Game

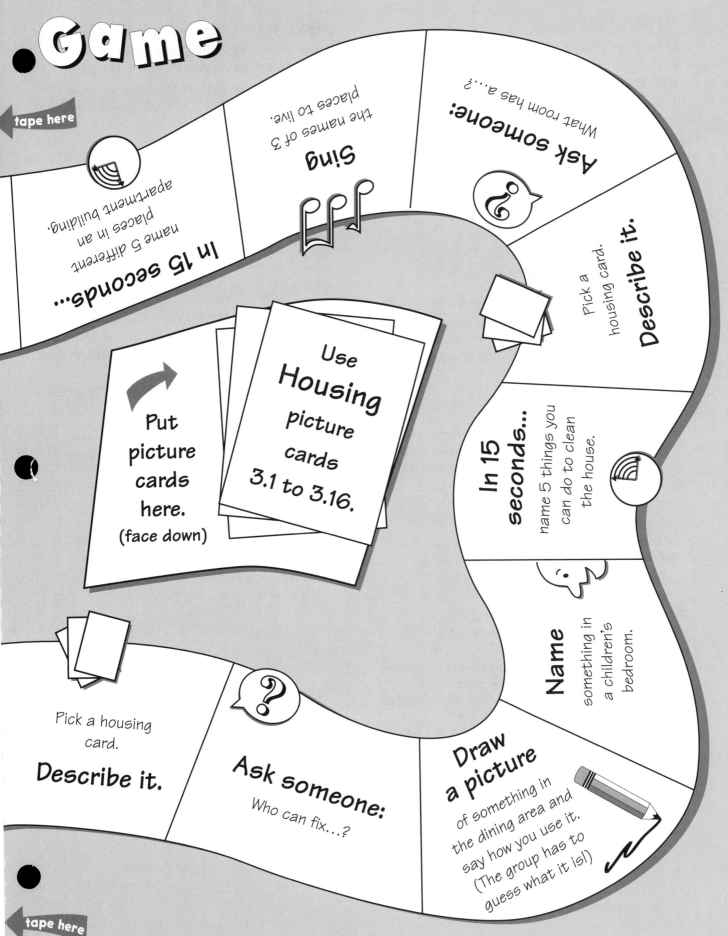

tape here

In 15 seconds...
name 5 different places in an apartment building.

Sing
the names of 5 places to live.

Ask someone:
What room has a...?

Describe it.
Pick a housing card.

Put picture cards here. (face down)

Use **Housing** picture cards 3.1 to 3.16.

In 15 seconds...
name 5 things you can do to clean the house.

Name
something in a children's bedroom.

Pick a housing card.
Describe it.

Ask someone:
Who can fix...?

Draw a picture
of something in the dining area and say how you use it. (The group has to guess what it is!)

tape here

Housing Picture Card Activities

TWIN GRIDS (Pairs)

Living Room/Dining Area/Kitchen Picture Cards, page 49

Grid, page 197

1. Duplicate one copy of the grid on page 197, and number each square 1–16. These are the aisles of a large discount store. Give each student one grid and one picture card page.

2. Have students cut apart their picture cards and place them face up and spread out on their desks next to the grid.

3. Tell students, *The ceiling fans are in Aisle 13.* Direct students to place the picture of a ceiling fan on square 13. Encourage students to ask clarification questions. *What aisle? Did you say ceiling fans?*

4. Continue telling students where all the items in the store are until all the grid squares are filled. Have students compare their grids with one another as you clarify any discrepancies.

5. Next, pair students. Give each pair a manila folder to use as a screen between the partners. Have the sender tell the receiver the location of the items in the store. (Students do not have to use the same sentences you used.) Both partners place their pictures on the grids. When the grids are complete, senders and receivers compare their grids.

6. Have senders and receivers switch roles.

PICK A PAIR (Pairs)

Yard and Housework Picture Cards, page 50
Yard Tools/Cleaning Supplies Picture Cards, page 51

1. Pair students and give each pair one picture card page.

2. Have students cut up cards, shuffle them, and place them face down on the desk in 4 rows of 8 cards.

3. Have partners take turns turning over two cards at a time, trying to match a cleaning action with a cleaning item. A student keeps the cards when she can make a sentence using both cards, for example, *I use dishwashing liquid to wash the dishes.* If the student can't say the sentence or the cards don't match, the student turns the cards back over.

4. The activity ends when all the matches have been made.

GUESS WHAT? (Pairs or Small Groups)

Yard and Housework Picture Cards, page 50
Yard Tools/Cleaning Supplies Picture Cards, page 51

1. Have each pair or group of students cut up one page of picture cards and place them face down on the desk.

2. Each student takes a turn picking up one card and giving a definition. *This is what gardeners do to a lawn.* (mow the lawn) The partner(s) try to guess the item from the definition.

3. The first student to correctly guess the item keeps the card.

4. The activity ends when all the cards are guessed correctly.

MIXER (Whole Class)

Household Problems/Repair People Picture Cards, page 52

1. Duplicate enough copies of the picture card page so that each student gets one card.

2. Give half of the students household problem cards and the other half worker cards. Have all the "people with household problems" go to one side of the room and all the "workers" go to the other.

3. Have students with problems go up to the workers and try to find a worker to fix the problem.

    My sink is leaking? Can you fix it?

    Yes, I can. I'm a plumber. OR

    I'm sorry. I'm a roofer, not a plumber.

4. When students find their partners, they can negotiate a price for the repairs.

5. The activity ends when everyone finds the correct worker.

Picture Cards: Living Room/Dining Area/Kitchen

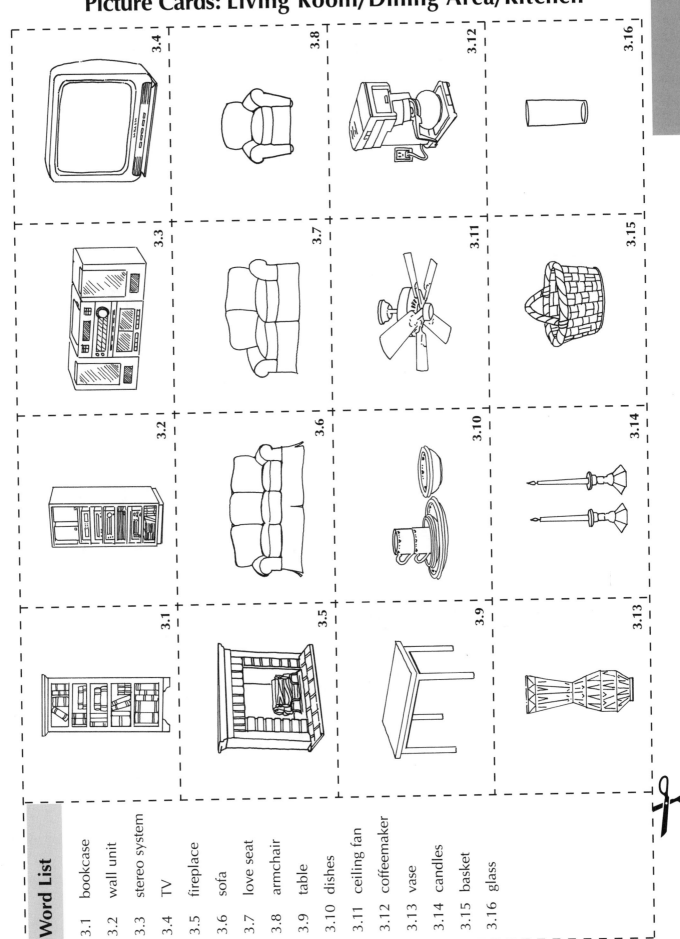

Picture Cards: Yard and Housework

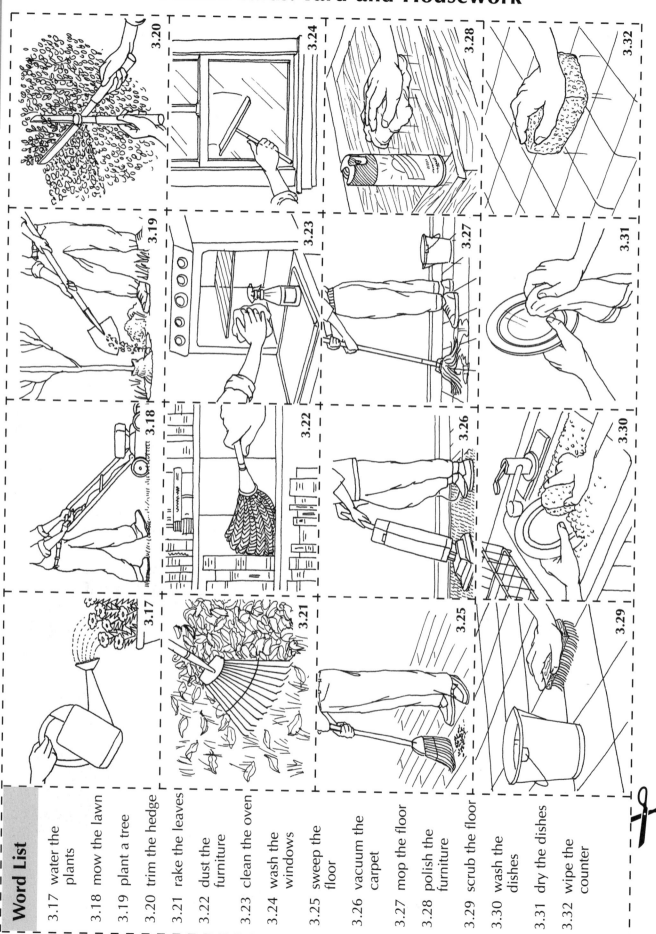

3.20
3.24
3.28
3.32
3.19
3.23
3.27
3.31
3.18
3.22
3.26
3.30
3.17
3.21
3.25
3.29

Word List

3.17 water the plants

3.18 mow the lawn

3.19 plant a tree

3.20 trim the hedge

3.21 rake the leaves

3.22 dust the furniture

3.23 clean the oven

3.24 wash the windows

3.25 sweep the floor

3.26 vacuum the carpet

3.27 mop the floor

3.28 polish the furniture

3.29 scrub the floor

3.30 wash the dishes

3.31 dry the dishes

3.32 wipe the counter

Picture Cards: Yard Tools/Cleaning Supplies

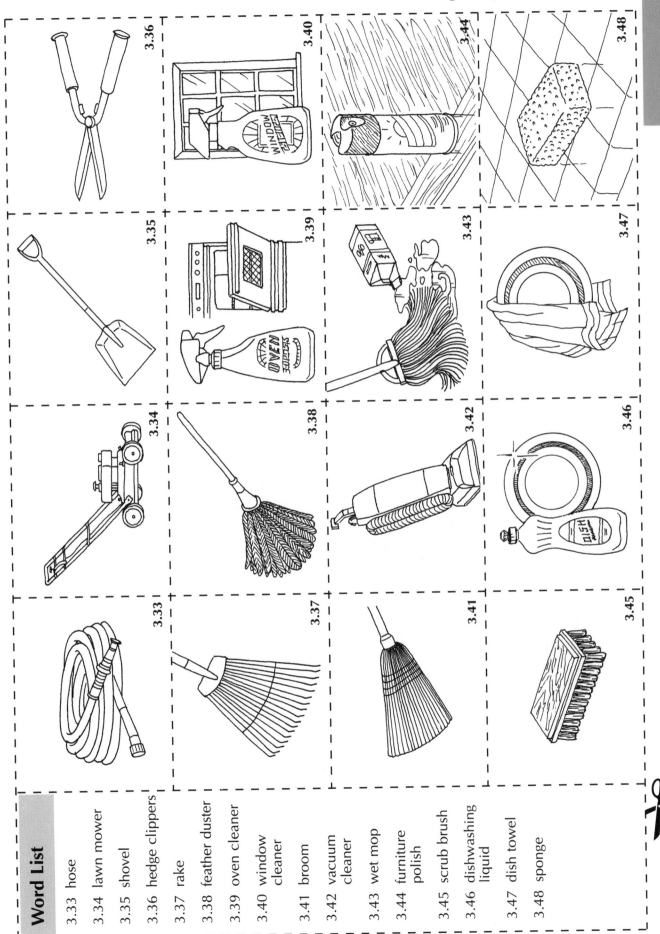

3.36

3.40

3.44

3.48

3.35

3.39

3.43

3.47

3.34

3.38

3.42

3.46

3.33

3.37

3.41

3.45

Word List

3.33 hose
3.34 lawn mower
3.35 shovel
3.36 hedge clippers
3.37 rake
3.38 feather duster
3.39 oven cleaner
3.40 window cleaner
3.41 broom
3.42 vacuum cleaner
3.43 wet mop
3.44 furniture polish
3.45 scrub brush
3.46 dishwashing liquid
3.47 dish towel
3.48 sponge

Picture Cards: Household Problems/Repair People

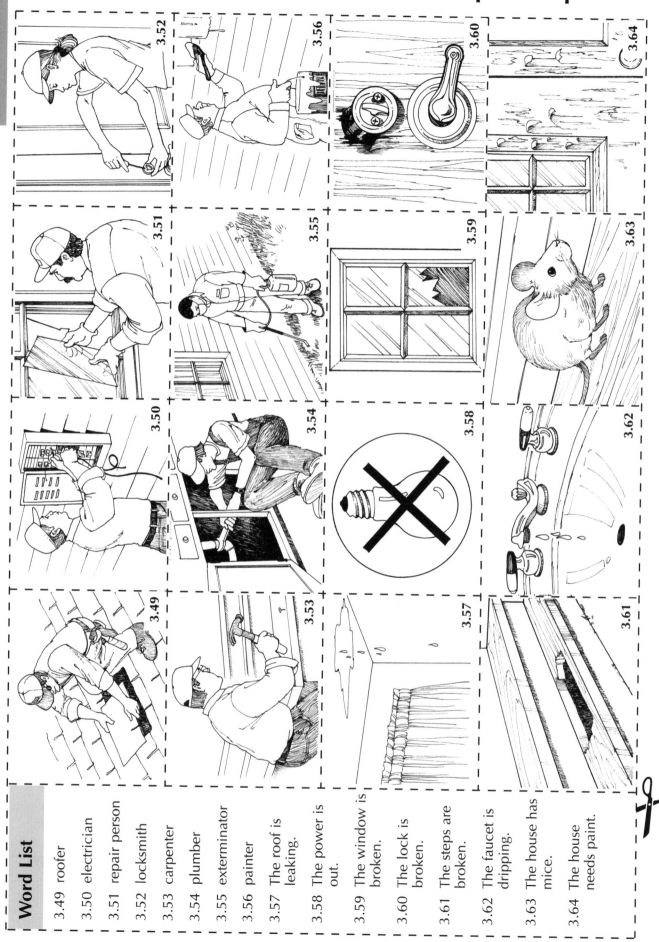

Word List

3.49 roofer
3.50 electrician
3.51 repair person
3.52 locksmith
3.53 carpenter
3.54 plumber
3.55 exterminator
3.56 painter
3.57 The roof is leaking.
3.58 The power is out.
3.59 The window is broken.
3.60 The lock is broken.
3.61 The steps are broken.
3.62 The faucet is dripping.
3.63 The house has mice.
3.64 The house needs paint.

4. Food

Page(s)		Fruit (50)	Vegetables (51)	Meat and Poultry (52)	Deli and Seafood (53)	The Market (54–55)	Containers and Packaged Foods (56)	Weights and Measures (57)	Food Preparation (58)	Kitchen Utensils (59)	Fast Food (60)	A Coffee Shop Menu (61)	A Restaurant (62–63)
54	**What's in the fridge?** (Round Table Label)	◆	◆	◆	◆	◆	◆						
55	**What do you want for dinner?** (Survey)			◆	◆	◆			◆			◆	
56–57	**How much do I need?** (Information Exchange)	◆				◆	◆	◆	◆	◆			
58–59	**What goes where?** (Drawing Dictation)												◆
60	**Don't forget the pasta!** (Role Play)	◆	◆	◆	◆	◆	◆	◆					
61	**Home–cooked Meals or Fast Food?** (Take a Stand)										◆	◆	
62–63	**Food Board Game** (Board Game)	◆	◆	◆	◆	◆	◆	◆	◆	◆	◆	◆	◆
64–68	**Picture Card Activities and Picture Cards**	◆	◆	◆	◆	◆	◆	◆	◆	◆	◆		◆

What's in the fridge?

The Oxford Picture Dictionary, pages 50–56. See page xii for Teacher's Notes.

◆ **Form groups of 4 people.**

◆ **Each person in the group takes turns labeling the food on this paper.**

◆ **After all the pictures have labels, look in the *Dictionary* to check your group's work.**

bananas

◆ **What's next?** Your teacher will draw an open refrigerator on the chalkboard. Take turns telling student volunteers what to draw on the shelves or in the door.

What do you want for dinner?

The Oxford Picture Dictionary, pages 52–55, 58, 61. See page xiv for Teacher's Notes.

Survey

- ◆ **Read the survey questions and mark your answers with a ✔.**
- ◆ **Ask and answer the questions again with nine classmates.**
- ◆ **Mark your classmates' answers on the survey.**

Do you prefer...

		My Answers	My Classmates' Answers	No Opinion
...roasted or fried chicken?	a. roasted			
	b. fried			
...cooked or raw carrots?	a. cooked			
	b. raw			
...mashed or baked potatoes?	a. mashed			
	b. baked			
...white or wheat bread?	a. white			
	b. wheat			
...fresh or canned fruit?	a. fresh			
	b. canned			
...orange or apple juice?	a. orange			
	b. apple			

- ◆ **Complete the graph below. Chart only student preferences.**

[a | b] (Note: Your chart will not show the "No Opinion" category.)

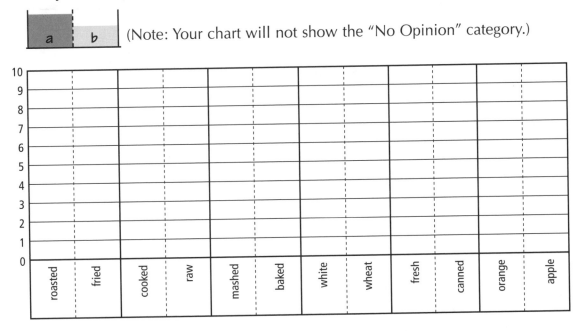

- ◆ **What's next?** Your teacher will survey the whole class. Write sentences about the answers. Follow the example below:

    More students prefer turkey hot dogs to beef hot dogs.

How much do I need?

The Oxford Picture Dictionary, pages 50, 54–59. See page xviii for Teacher's Notes.

Information Exchange

A

1

- ◆ Sit with a partner. (Don't show this paper to your partner!)
- ◆ Ask your partner about the missing information in the recipe below.
- ◆ You can use these questions:

    "How much _____ do I need?" or *"How many _____ do I need?"*

    "What do I do with the _____ ?"

- ◆ Write in the missing information and read it back to your partner to check your work.

COCOA-COCONUT-BERRY BALLS (makes 50 cookies)

_____ vanilla wafers   _____ jam

_____ powdered sugar   _____ chopped nuts

_____ cocoa   _____ shredded coconut

1. Crush the vanilla wafers and put them in a large bowl.
2. _____ the cocoa to the wafers.
3. _____ the coconut, jam and chopped nuts.
4. Make small balls of the mixture and put them on a plate.
5. Cocoa-Coconut-Berry Balls can stay in the refrigerator for a _____ .

2

- ◆ Use the recipe below to answer your partner's questions.

FRUIT SALAD (serves 6)

1/2 lb. grapes   3 peaches or pears

3 apples   1 15-oz. can sliced pineapple

1/2 c. yogurt   1/4 c. raisins

1. Wash all the fruit.
2. Chop the apples.
3. Slice the peaches or pears.
4. Cut up the pineapple into bite-size pieces.
5. Put all the fruit into a large bowl.
6. Mix in the yogurt and add the raisins.
7. Refrigerate for 1/2 hour. Serves six.

- ◆ **What's next?** Decide which of these recipes you want to prepare in class. Discuss what utensils and ingredients you will need. Invite other teachers, your principal, or office staff to sample your recipe.

How much do I need?

B

 1

♦ **Sit with a partner. (Don't show this paper to your partner!)**

♦ **Use the recipe below to answer your partner's questions.**

COCOA-COCONUT-BERRY BALLS (makes 50 cookies)

2 c. vanilla wafers　　　3 Tbs. jam
1/2 c. powdered sugar　　1/4 c. chopped nuts
3 Tbs. cocoa　　　　　　1/2 c. shredded coconut

1. Crush the vanilla wafers and put them in a large bowl.
2. Add the cocoa to the wafers.
3. Mix in the coconut, jam and chopped nuts.
4. Make small balls of the mixture and put them on a plate.
5. Cocoa-Coconut-Berry Balls can stay in the refrigerator for a week.

2

♦ **Ask your partner about the missing information on the recipe below.**

♦ **You can use these questions:**

"How much _____ do I need?" or "How many _____ do I need?"

"What do I do with the _____ ?"

♦ **Write in the missing information and read it back to your partner to check your work.**

FRUIT SALAD (serves 6)

_____ grapes　　　　　_____ peaches or pears
_____ apples　　　　　_____ sliced pineapple
_____ yogurt　　　　　_____ raisins

1. Wash all the fruit.
2. _____ the apples.
3. _____ the peaches or pears.
4. _____ the pineapple into bite-size pieces.
5. Put all the fruit into a large bowl.
6. _____ in the yogurt and _____ the raisins.
7. Refrigerate for 1/2 hour. Serves six.

♦ **What's next?** Decide which of these recipes you want to prepare in class. Discuss what utensils and ingredients you will need. Invite other teachers, your principal, or office staff to sample your recipe.

　　　　　Unit Four　57

What goes where?

Drawing Dictation

A

 1

- ◆ **Sit with a partner. (Don't show this paper to your partner!)**
- ◆ **Describe the table setting at Fifi's Restaurant.**
- ◆ **Your partner will draw what you say.**
- ◆ **Answer your partner's questions.**

 2

- ◆ **Listen to your partner describe a table setting at Candy's Coffee Shop and draw what you hear.**
- ◆ **These questions may help:**

   "Did you say __fork__?" "Is that <u>on the __left__</u> or on the __right__?"

- ◆ **When both pictures are complete, compare your work.**

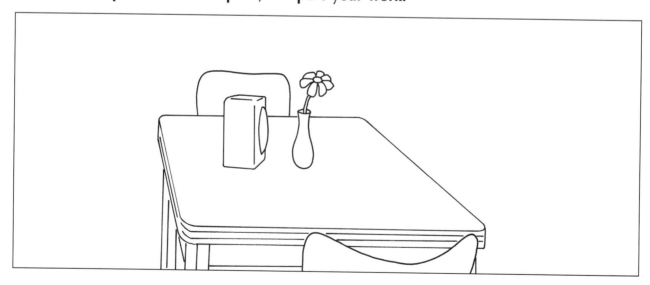

- ◆ **What's next?** Describe a table setting to your teacher. Your teacher will draw what you say. Correct your teacher's mistakes.

What goes where?

The Oxford Picture Dictionary, pages 62–63. See page xv for Teacher's Notes.

Drawing Dictation

B

1

- ◆ **Sit with a partner. (Don't show this paper to your partner!)**
- ◆ **Listen to your partner describe a table setting at Fifi's Restaurant and draw what you hear.**
- ◆ **These questions may help:**

    *"Did you say **fork**?"* *"Is that <u>on the **left**</u> or <u>on the **right**</u>?"*

2

- ◆ **Describe the table setting at Candy's Coffee Shop.**
- ◆ **Your partner will draw what you say.**
- ◆ **Answer your partner's questions.**
- ◆ **When both pictures are complete, compare your work.**

- ◆ **What's next?** Describe a table setting to your teacher. Your teacher will draw what you say. Correct your teacher's mistakes.

Don't forget the pasta!

The Oxford Picture Dictionary, pages 50–57. See page xix for Teacher's Notes.

Role Play

- ◆ Form groups of 4 people.
- ◆ Practice saying all the lines.
- ◆ Choose your character and decide what you will say.
- ◆ Think of other things your character can say.
- ◆ Act out your role play.

THE SCENE:
A family is sitting in their kitchen. They're making their grocery list.

THE CHARACTERS:
a mom
a dad
a teenager
a little kid

THE PROPS:
empty food boxes
empty containers
paper
a pencil

THE SCRIPT:

Who says...	...these lines?
Mom	We need to get a <u>loaf of bread</u>*.
	We also need to pick up some <u>spaghetti</u>.
	That's a great idea! Let's get <u>garlic</u> too.
	Why don't we buy some <u>rice</u>?
	We already have a <u>box of rice</u>.
	Oh, don't forget <u>carrots</u>. I love <u>carrots</u>.
	I don't eat <u>carrots</u>. I hate <u>them</u>!
	Please put <u>candy bars</u> on the list!
	No way. We're not buying <u>sweets</u>!
	Let's put <u>seafood</u> on the list.
	You can buy it, but I won't eat it.
	Yech! Why are we buying that?

*You can substitute other vocabulary for the underlined words.

- ◆ **What's next?** Plan a dinner that all four of these people will like. Include a salad, a main dish, a side dish, a dessert, and a beverage.

Home-Cooked Meals or Fast Food?

The Oxford Picture Dictionary, pages 60–61. See page xx for Teacher's Notes.

Take a Stand

● ◆ **Think about the reasons to eat home-cooked meals or fast food.**

◆ **Read each statement on the list.**

◆ **If the statement shows that <u>eating home-cooked meals</u> is a good idea, make a ✓ in that column.**

◆ **If the statement shows that <u>eating fast food</u> is a good idea, make a ✓ in that column.**

◆ **For K and L, think of two more statements to add to this list.**

STATEMENTS	Home-Cooked	Fast Food
A. You can make a home-cooked meal for four for less than $10.00.		
B. You can prepare meals quickly in a microwave.		
C. Dinner is a time when people who live together can talk.		
D. Fast food restaurants are adding low-fat foods to their menus.		
E. Everyone can order a different meal in a restaurant.		
F. Fast food restaurants often close at 10:00 or 11:00 at night.		
G. You can't see what happens in the kitchen in most restaurants.		
H. You don't have to cook or clean up when you eat in a restaurant.		
I. You have to wear shirts and shoes in a fast food restaurant.		
J. You often have leftovers when you cook at home.		
K.		
L.		

◆ **Sit with a partner and compare papers.**

◆ **Write your and your partner's ideas.**

I think it is better to eat _____ *because* _____

_____ .

My partner thinks it is better to eat _____ *because* _____

_____ .

● ◆ **What's next?** Take a stand. Your teacher will tell you where to stand if you support home-cooked meals, and where to stand if you support fast food.

Food Board

tape here →

Draw
a place setting and describe what you've drawn.

Name
3 sections in the market.

Pick a fruit and vegetables card. Say 3 things about it.

Answer:
Do you prefer paper or plastic shopping bags? Why?

In 15 seconds...
name 5 different restaurant jobs.

Act out
a cooking verb for your group. (The group has to guess what it is!)

To begin...

- Put your markers on start.
- Take turns flipping a coin to move your marker around the board.

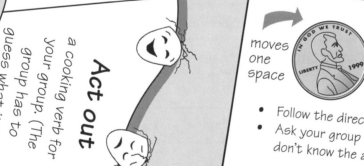

moves one space

moves two spaces

- Follow the directions on the squares.
- Ask your group for help when you don't know the answer.

FINISH

Start

Pick a fruit and vegetables card.
Spell it.

Name
something you eat every day.

tape here →

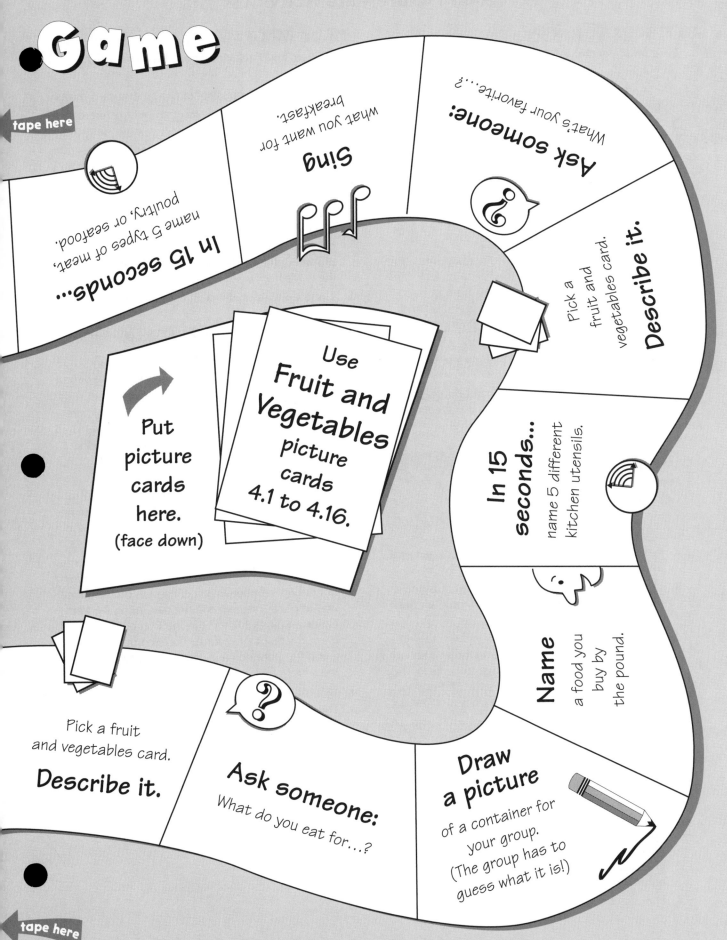

Game

tape here

In 15 seconds...
name 5 types of meat, poultry, or seafood.

Sing
what you want for breakfast.

Ask someone:
What's your favorite...?

Describe it.
Pick a fruit and vegetables card.

Put picture cards here.
(face down)

Use Fruit and Vegetables picture cards 4.1 to 4.16.

In 15 seconds...
name 5 different kitchen utensils.

Name
a food you buy by the pound.

Describe it.
Pick a fruit and vegetables card.

Ask someone:
What do you eat for...?

Draw a picture
of a container for your group. (The group has to guess what it is!)

tape here

© 1999 Oxford University Press   Permission granted to reproduce for classroom use.

Unit Four   63

Food Picture Card Activities

PEER DICTATION (Pairs)

Fruit and Vegetables Picture Cards, page 65

1. Duplicate a class set of the picture card pages and cut off the Word List on the sidebar. (Hold on to these for step 6.)

2. Pair students and give student A the picture card page.

3. Direct the B students to look at page 50 in the *Dictionary* and read off the list of fruits. When the A students hear a fruit that is on their picture page they say, *I have that. How do you spell it?* B students spell out the word so that the A's can write it under the picture.

4. When the A's have written all the fruit words, they put their papers aside. B's then get a picture card page and listen to A's read the list from page 51. They request the spelling of the vegetables and write them under the pictures on their pages.

5. Once the B's have finished, have the A's close their dictionaries. Partners can then work together to label their respective pages.

6. As a final check for accuracy, hand out the Word Lists you put aside in step 1 so that students can check their spelling.

TWIN GRIDS (Pairs)

Market/Prepared Foods Picture Cards, page 66
Grid, page 197

1. Duplicate one copy of the grid on page 197 and write in 16 short names, one name per square. (Sam, Tom, Kim, etc.) Give each student one grid and one picture card page.

2. Have students cut apart their picture cards and place them face up and spread out, on their desks next to the grid.

3. Tell students that *Sam likes chicken.* Direct students to place the picture of chicken on the grid square with Sam's name in it. Encourage students to ask clarification questions, for example, *Did you say Sam? Chicken or cheese? What does he like? etc.*

4. Continue telling students who likes what until all the grid squares are filled. Have students compare their grids with one another as you clarify any discrepancies.

5. Next, pair students. Give each pair a manila folder to use as a screen between the partners. Have the sender tell the receiver what Sam likes. (Students do not have to copy your sentences.) Both partners place their pictures on the grids. When the grids are complete, senders and receivers compare their grids.

6. Have senders and receivers switch roles.

PICK A PAIR (Pairs)

Containers and Packaged Foods Picture Cards, page 67

1. Duplicate 1/2 a class set of the picture card pages.

2. Pair students and give each pair one picture card page.

3. Have the pair cut up the cards, shuffle them, and place them face down in four rows of four cards.

4. Have partners take turns turning over two cards at a time, trying to match containers with food items. When the cards match for example, *bottle* and *soda*, the student keeps the cards if she can say the phrase *A bottle of soda.* If the student can't say the phrase, or the cards don't match, the student turns the cards back over and the next student goes.

5. The activity ends when all the cards are gone.

NOW AND THEN CHARADES (Groups)

Food Verbs Picture Cards, page 68

1. Duplicate one picture card page for each group of 4-5 students.

2. Group students and give each group one picture card page. Tell students to number off. Have #1 cut apart the picture cards. Have #2 shuffle the cards and place them face down on a desk. Identify #4 as the recorder.

3. For the first round, Student #1 picks a card from the deck, asks *What am I doing?*, and pantomimes the action until the group can name it. Once the group names the action: *You're setting the table*, student #1 sits down.

4. The recorder then asks the group, *What did Carlos do?* Group members reach consensus on the correct way to put the sentence in the past, using the **Verb Guide** on pages 170–172 in the *Dictionary* to check the correct past tense form. The recorder writes the group's response on a sheet of paper, e.g., *Carlos set the table.*

5. Student #2 picks a card and the activity continues.

6. The activity is over when all the students in the group have had two turns. The recorder can read from or turn in the paper.

Picture Cards: Fruit and Vegetables

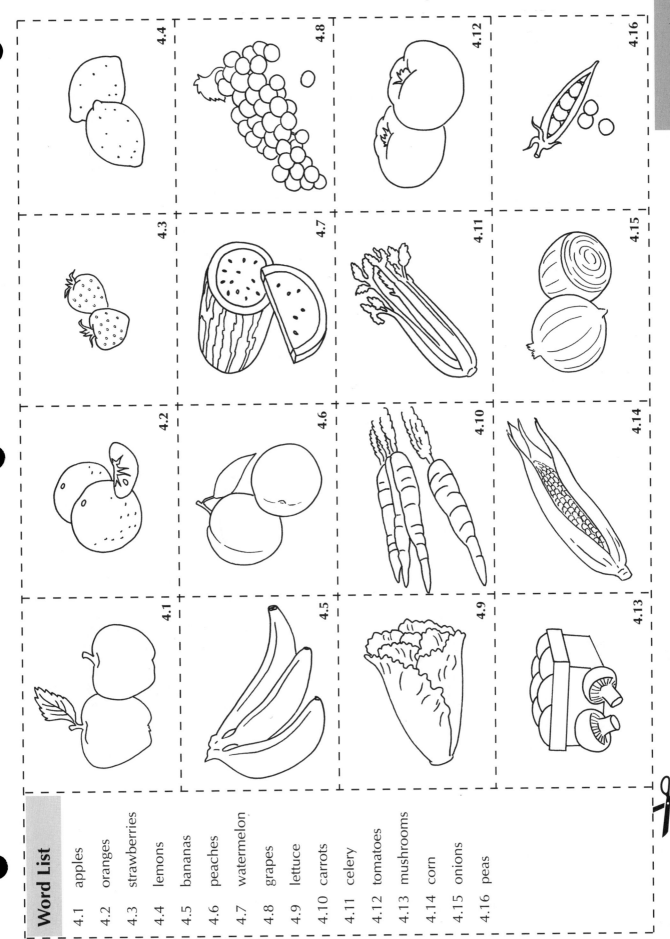

4.4	4.8	4.12	4.16
4.3	4.7	4.11	4.15
4.2	4.6	4.10	4.14
4.1	4.5	4.9	4.13

Word List

4.1 apples
4.2 oranges
4.3 strawberries
4.4 lemons
4.5 bananas
4.6 peaches
4.7 watermelon
4.8 grapes
4.9 lettuce
4.10 carrots
4.11 celery
4.12 tomatoes
4.13 mushrooms
4.14 corn
4.15 onions
4.16 peas

Picture Cards: Market/Prepared Foods

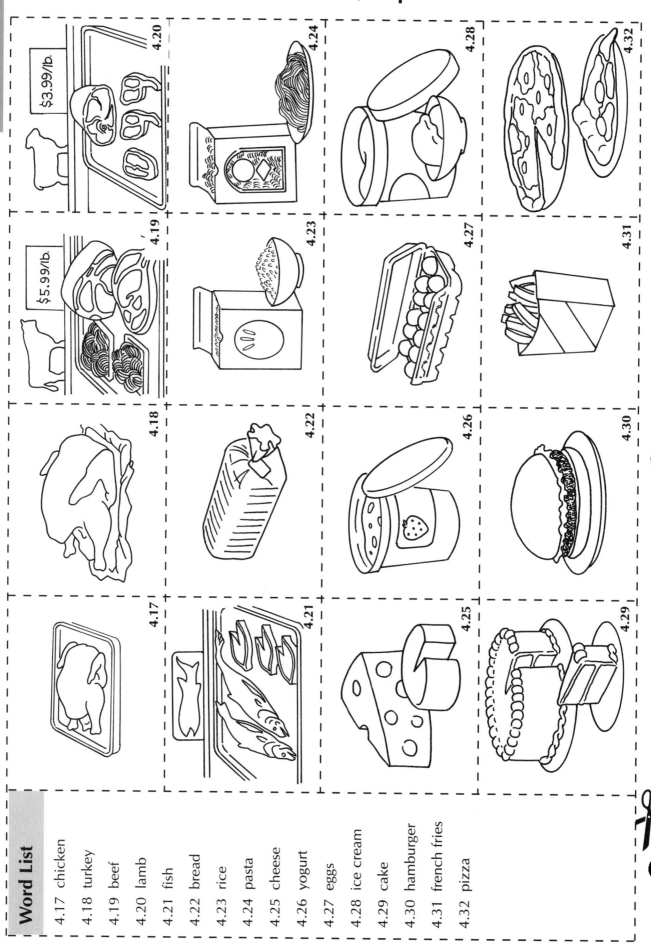

© 1999 Oxford University Press   Permission granted to reproduce for classroom use.

Picture Cards: Containers and Packaged Foods

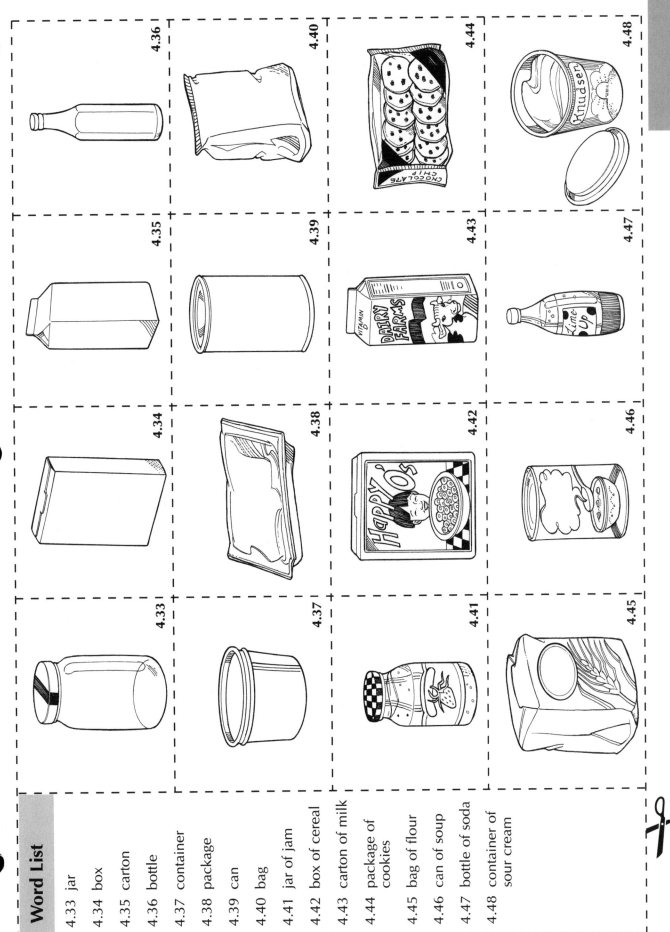

4.36

4.40

4.44

4.48

4.35

4.39

4.43

4.47

4.34

4.38

4.42

4.46

4.33

4.37

4.41

4.45

Word List

4.33 jar
4.34 box
4.35 carton
4.36 bottle
4.37 container
4.38 package
4.39 can
4.40 bag
4.41 jar of jam
4.42 box of cereal
4.43 carton of milk
4.44 package of cookies
4.45 bag of flour
4.46 can of soup
4.47 bottle of soda
4.48 container of sour cream

Picture Cards: Food Verbs

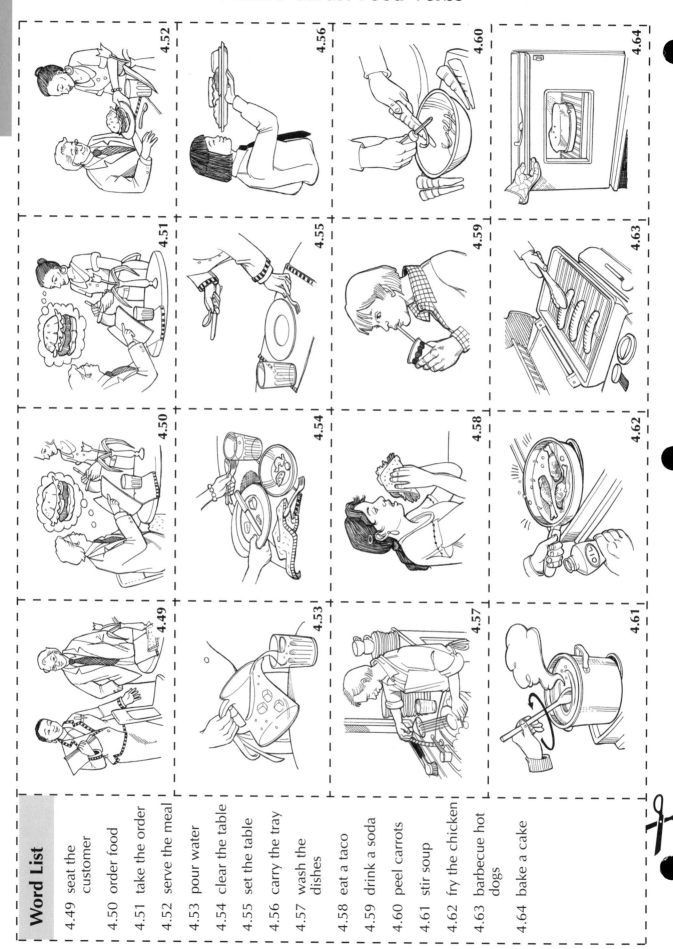

| | | | 4.52 | | | | 4.56 | | | | 4.60 | | | | 4.64 |

| | | | 4.51 | | | | 4.55 | | | | 4.59 | | | | 4.63 |

| | | | 4.50 | | | | 4.54 | | | | 4.58 | | | | 4.62 |

| | | | 4.49 | | | | 4.53 | | | | 4.57 | | | | 4.61 |

Word List

4.49 seat the customer
4.50 order food
4.51 take the order
4.52 serve the meal
4.53 pour water
4.54 clear the table
4.55 set the table
4.56 carry the tray
4.57 wash the dishes
4.58 eat a taco
4.59 drink a soda
4.60 peel carrots
4.61 stir soup
4.62 fry the chicken
4.63 barbecue hot dogs
4.64 bake a cake

5. Clothing

Page(s)		Clothing I (64–65)	Clothing II (66)	Clothing III (67)	Shoes and Accessories (68–69)	Describing Clothes (70–71)	Doing the Laundry (72)	Sewing and Alterations (73)
70	**Family Fashion** (Round Table Label)	♦	♦	♦	♦			
71	**What's your style?** (Survey)	♦	♦		♦			
72–73	**Life at the Laundromat** (Picture Differences)						♦	
74–75	**Wash and Wear Opposites** (Double Crossword)					♦	♦	♦
76	**Lacy's Fine Fashions** (Role Play)	♦	♦	♦	♦	♦		♦
77	**School Uniforms–Yes or No?** (Take a Stand)	♦	♦			♦		
78–79	**Clothing Board Game** (Board Game)	♦	♦	♦	♦	♦	♦	♦
80–84	**Picture Card Activities and Picture Cards**	♦	♦	♦	♦	♦		♦

Family Fashion

The Oxford Picture Dictionary, pages 64–69. See page xii for Teacher's Notes.

- ◆ Form groups of 4 people.
- ◆ Each person in the group takes turns labeling the clothing items on this paper.
- ◆ After all the pictures have labels, look in the *Dictionary* to check your group's work.

sports shirt

- ◆ **What's next?** Your teacher will draw several stick figures on the chalkboard. Take turns telling student volunteers what clothing items to draw on them.

What's your style?

The Oxford Picture Dictionary, pages 64–66, 70–71. See page xiv for Teacher's Notes.

Survey

- ◆ **Read the survey questions and mark your answers with a ✔.**
- ◆ **Ask and answer the questions again with nine classmates.**
- ◆ **Mark your classmates' answers on the survey form.**

Do you prefer...

		My Answers	My Classmates' Answers	No Opinion
...long-sleeved or short-sleeved shirts?	a. long-sleeved			
	b. short-sleeved			
...pullover or cardigan sweaters?	a. pullover			
	b. cardigan			
...solid or print T-shirts?	a. solid			
	b. print			
...jeans or slacks?	a. jeans			
	b. slacks			
...jackets or coats?	a. jackets			
	b. coats			
...mittens or gloves?	a. mittens			
	b. gloves			

- ◆ **Complete the graph below. Chart only student preferences.**

a	b

(Note: Your chart will not show the "No Opinion" category.)

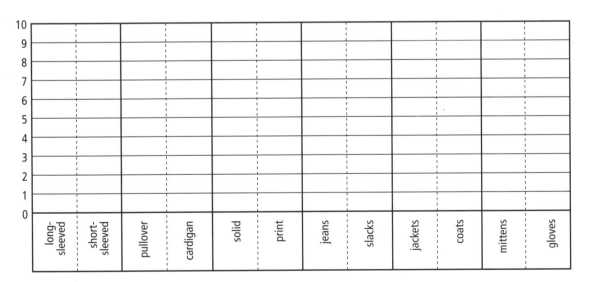

- ◆ **What's next?** Your teacher will survey the whole class. Write sentences about the answers. Follow the example below:

  Most students prefer long-sleeved shirts to short-sleeved shirts.

Life at the Laundromat

The Oxford Picture Dictionary, page 72. See page xvi for Teacher's Notes.

Picture Differences

A

- ◆ Sit with a partner and look at each other's papers.
- ◆ There are 10 differences between your pictures.
- ◆ Work with your partner to find the differences.

- ◆ Write the differences you find on the chart below.

A	B
1. laundry basket on floor	laundry basket on dryer
2.	
3.	
4.	
5.	
6.	
7.	
8.	
9.	
10.	

Life at the Laundromat

The Oxford Picture Dictionary, page 72. See page xvi for Teacher's Notes..

◆ **Sit with a partner and look at each other's papers.**

◆ **There are 10 differences between your pictures.**

◆ **Work with your partner to find the differences.**

◆ **Write the differences you find on the chart below.**

A	B
1. laundry basket on floor	laundry basket on dryer
2.	
3.	
4.	
5.	
6.	
7.	
8.	
9.	
10.	

Wash and Wear Opposites

The Oxford Picture Dictionary, pages 70–73. See page xvii for Teacher's Notes.

◆ **Sit with a partner. (Don't show this paper to your partner!)**

◆ **Take turns giving the clues to complete the puzzle.**

   1 down—This uniform isn't ironed. It's….

◆ **If your partner needs help, give one letter from the answer on your puzzle.**

   The first letter is W.

◆ **When both puzzles are complete, compare your work.**

Clues

1 down — This uniform isn't ironed. It's…

2 down — These shoes aren't new. They're…

4 down — These jeans aren't baggy. They're…

6 down — This belt isn't wide. It's…

7 down — This zipper isn't working. It's…

9 down — This button isn't on the shirt. It's…

12 down — This blouse isn't plain. It's…

15 down — These heels aren't high. They're…

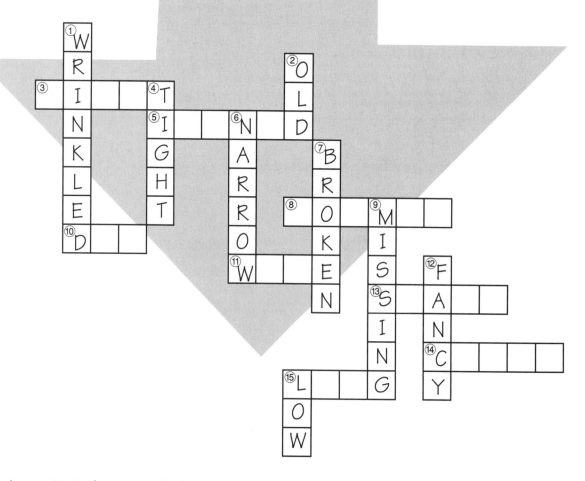

◆ **What's next?** Find two words that have opposites in the puzzle. Write a sentence using each word.

Wash and Wear Opposites

The Oxford Picture Dictionary, pages 70–73. See page xvii for Teacher's Notes.

Double Crossword

B

- ◆ **Sit with a partner. (Don't show this paper to your partner!)**
- ◆ **Take turns giving the clues to complete the puzzle.**

    3 across —This jacket isn't heavy. It's…

- ◆ **If your partner needs help, give one letter from the answer on your puzzle.**

    The first letter is L.

- ◆ **When both puzzles are complete, compare your work.**

Clues

3 across — This jacket isn't heavy. It's…

5 across — This shirt isn't wrinkled. It's…

8 across — This dress isn't casual. It's…

10 across — This laundry isn't wet. It's…

11 across — This tie isn't narrow. It's…

13 across — These overalls aren't big. They're…

14 across — This T-shirt isn't dirty. It's…

15 across — These sleeves aren't short. They're…

- ◆ **What's next?** Find two words that have opposites in the puzzle. Write a sentence using each word.

Lacy's Fine Fashions

The Oxford Picture Dictionary, pages 64–71, 73. See page xix for Teacher's Notes.

Role Play

- ◆ Form groups of 3–4 people.
- ◆ Practice saying all the lines.
- ◆ Choose your character and decide what you will say.
- ◆ Think of other things your character can say.
- ◆ Act out your role play.

THE SCENE:
a men's
and women's
clothing store

THE CHARACTERS:
one or two customers
a salesclerk
a tailor or
a dressmaker

THE PROPS:
clothing items and accessories
(shirt, pants, sweater)
a few sewing items
(tape measure, pin cushion,
needle and thread)

THE SCRIPT:

Who says...	...these lines?
a customer	Where can I try on these jeans*?
	A silver chain would look nice with that sweater.
	We charge extra to sew silk clothing.
	Do you have this striped shirt in a large?
	Right away. I'll get my tape measure.
	That style is popular now. All our overalls are baggy.
	That jacket looks narrow. I can change that for you.
	This sleeve is too short. Can you lengthen it?
	Sorry, we're out of striped shirts. But we have solid ones.
	The fitting rooms are over by the suits.
	I don't repair sale items. Maybe there's another shirt in your size.
	This shirt has a missing button.

* You can substitute other vocabulary for the underlined words.

- ◆ **What's next?** Take a shopping trip. Look in the *Dictionary* and make a list of ten clothing or accessory items you would like to buy.

School Uniforms — Yes or No?

The Oxford Picture Dictionary, pages 64–66, 70–71. See page xx for Teacher's Notes.

Take a Stand

- ♦ **Think about the reasons to wear or not wear school uniforms.**
- ♦ **Read each statement on the list.**
- ♦ **If the statement shows that uniforms are <u>a good idea</u>, make a ✔ in that column.**
- ♦ **If the statement shows that uniforms are <u>not a good idea</u>, make a ✔ in that column.**
- ♦ **For K and L, think of two more statements to add to this list.**

STATEMENTS	+	−
A. Young people like to wear the latest fashion styles.		
B. You can save money by shopping at "back to school" sales.		
C. Students enjoy wearing special school colors.		
D. Some boys and girls don't want to decide what to wear each day.		
E. Gangs identify their members by special clothes or colors.		
F. Some teachers say their students act better in formal clothes.		
G. Some parents cannot afford to buy lots of different clothes.		
H. Many students don't like to wear the same style and color every day.		
I. Some kids feel bad if they don't have stylish clothes like their friends.		
J. Students can wear school clothes outside school.		
K.		
L.		

- ♦ **Sit with a partner and compare papers.**

- ♦ **Write your and your partner's ideas.**

I think it is a _____ *idea to wear school uniforms because* _____

_____ .

My partner thinks it is a _____ *idea to wear school uniforms because*

_____ .

- ♦ **What's next?** Take a stand. Your teacher will tell you where to stand if you support school uniforms and where to stand if you don't support school uniforms.

Clothing Board.

tape here

Draw
something in your closet.
Describe it.

Name
a type of sweater.

Pick a clothing card.
Say 3 things about it.

Answer:
What are you wearing today?

In 15 seconds...
name 3 different kinds of shoes.

Act out
a laundry verb for your group.
(The group has to guess what it is!)

To begin...
• Put your markers on start.
• Take turns flipping a coin to move your marker around the board.

moves one space

moves two spaces

• Follow the directions on the squares.
• Ask your group for help when you don't know the answer.

Finish!

Start
Pick a clothing card.
Spell it.

Name
a laundry product that you use.

tape here

Game

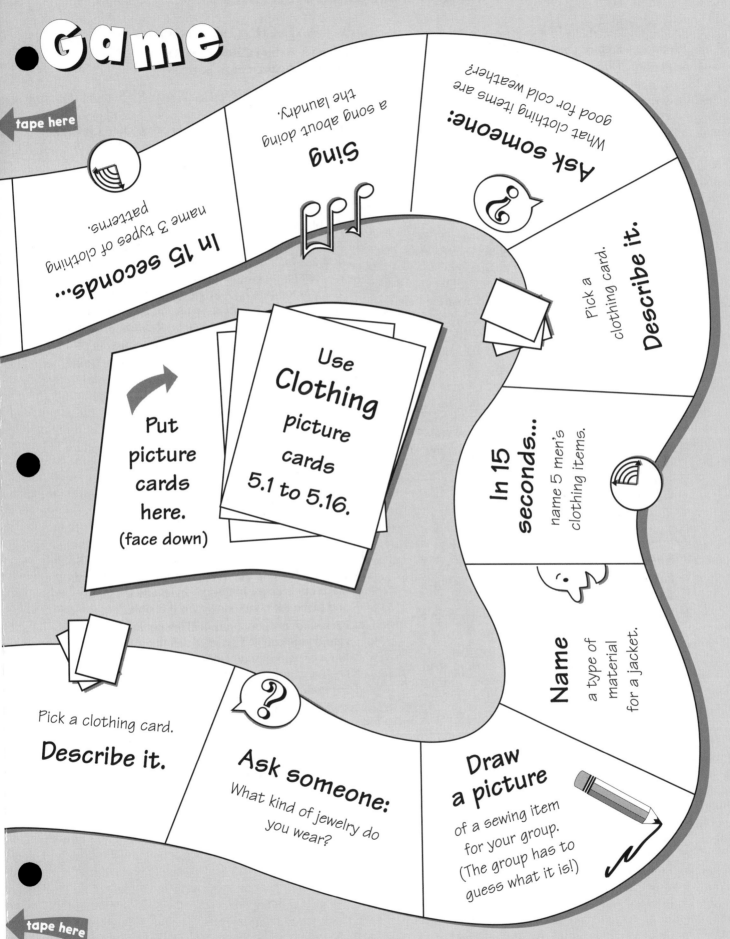

tape here

In 15 seconds... name 3 types of clothing patterns.

Sing a song about doing the laundry.

Ask someone: What clothing items are good for cold weather?

Pick a clothing card. **Describe it.**

Put picture cards here. (face down)

Use **Clothing** picture cards 5.1 to 5.16.

In 15 seconds... name 5 men's clothing items.

Name a type of material for a jacket.

Pick a clothing card. **Describe it.**

Ask someone: What kind of jewelry do you wear?

Draw a picture of a sewing item for your group. (The group has to guess what it is!)

tape here

Clothing Picture Card Activities

TWIN GRIDS (Pairs)

Clothing A Picture Cards, page 81
Grid, page 197

1. Duplicate one copy of the grid on page 197 and write in 16 short names, one name per square. (Sam, Tom, Kim, etc.) Give each student one grid and one picture card page. (If you have an overhead projector, see Using the Overhead Projector in the Picture Cards Teacher's Notes, page x.)

2. Have students cut apart their picture card page and place them face up and spread out, on their desks next to the grid.

3. Tell students that *Sam is wearing a shirt.* Direct students to place the picture of the shirt on the grid square with Sam's name on it. Encourage students to ask clarification questions. *Did you say Sam? Shirt or skirt? What's Sam wearing?*, etc.

4. Continue telling students who's wearing what clothes until all the grid squares are filled. Have students compare their grids with one another's as you clarify any discrepancies.

5. Next, pair students. Give each pair a manila folder to use as a screen between the partners. Have the sender tell the receiver what Kim is wearing. (Students do not have to copy your sentences.) Both partners place their pictures on the grids. When the grids are complete, senders and receivers compare their grids.

6. Have senders and receivers switch roles.

PICK A PAIR (Pairs)

Describing Clothes Picture Cards, page 82

1. Pair students and give each pair one picture card page.

2. Have the pair cut up the cards, shuffle them and place them face down in four rows of four cards.

3. Have partners take turns turning over two cards at a time, trying to match the same clothing item but with opposite descriptions. When the cards match, for example: new jeans/old jeans, the student keeps the cards if she can make a sentence comparing both pictures. *The new jeans look nice, but the old jeans have a rip.* If the student can't say the sentence or the cards don't match, (*new jeans/ long skirt*), the student turns the cards back over.

4. The activity ends when all the cards are gone.

PICK AND CHOOSE (Groups)

Clothing A Picture Cards, page 81
Clothing B Picture Cards, page 83

1. Duplicate one of each picture card page for each group of 2-4 students.

2. Give each group one copy of each picture card page and a piece of blank paper. Have them cut apart the pictures and place them in random rows, face up on the table.

3. Draw a large empty suitcase on the board and have one group member copy the picture onto the blank paper.

4. Announce the first round of play, indicating a destination and weather conditions. *We're taking a vacation in <u>Hawaii</u>. The weather is <u>hot</u>. We're going to the <u>beach</u>. Your group has two minutes to choose eight clothing items. Put them in your suitcase. Everyone must agree on the items you pick.*

5. Walk around, encouraging students to discuss their choices and monitering to make sure everyone has a chance to "pack the suitcase."

6. Call time and survey the class to find out the most popular clothing items. Continue play using different travel destinations.

7. To simplify the activity, use only one set of picture cards and limit the suitcase to five items.

GUESS WHAT? (Groups)

Sewing Items/Clothing Accessories Picture Cards, page 84

1. Have students form small groups of 2-4 students.

2. Give each group one page of cut-up picture cards. Have one student in the group shuffle the cards and place them face down on the table.

3. Each student takes a turn picking up the top picture card on the pile and giving a definition. *You use this to sew. It is very sharp.* (needle) Caution students not to use any part of the word in their definition. For example you can't say, *You measure clothes with this.* (tape measure)

4. The other group members try to guess the word. The first student to guess the word keeps the picture card.

5. The activity ends when all the cards are guessed correctly.

Picture Cards: Clothing A

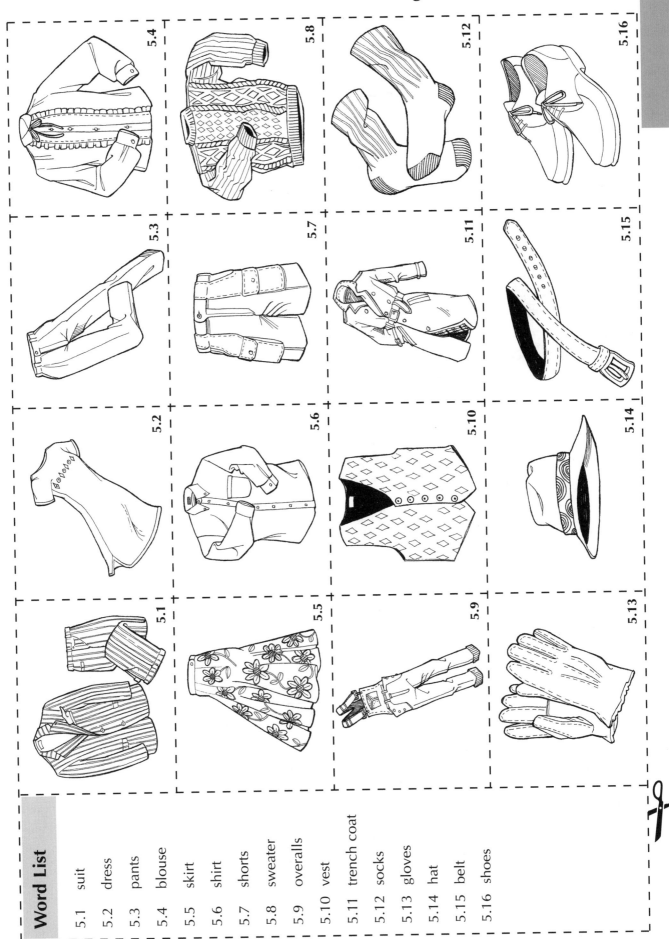

5.4

5.8

5.12

5.16

5.3

5.7

5.11

5.15

5.2

5.6

5.10

5.14

5.1

5.5

5.9

5.13

Word List

5.1 suit

5.2 dress

5.3 pants

5.4 blouse

5.5 skirt

5.6 shirt

5.7 shorts

5.8 sweater

5.9 overalls

5.10 vest

5.11 trench coat

5.12 socks

5.13 gloves

5.14 hat

5.15 belt

5.16 shoes

Picture Cards: Describing Clothes

5.20	5.24	5.28	5.32
5.19	5.23	5.27	5.31
5.18	5.22	5.26	5.30
5.17	5.21	5.25	5.29

Word List

5.17 new jeans
5.18 old jeans
5.19 long skirt
5.20 short skirt
5.21 plain blouse
5.22 fancy blouse
5.23 light jacket
5.24 heavy jacket
5.25 baggy pants
5.26 tight pants
5.27 wide tie
5.28 narrow tie
5.29 clean T-shirt
5.30 dirty T-shirt
5.31 wrinkled shirt
5.32 ironed shirt

Picture Cards: Clothing B

5.36	5.40	5.44	5.48
5.35	5.39	5.43	5.47
5.34	5.38	5.42	5.46
5.33	5.37	5.41	5.45

Picture Cards: Sewing Items/Clothing Accessories

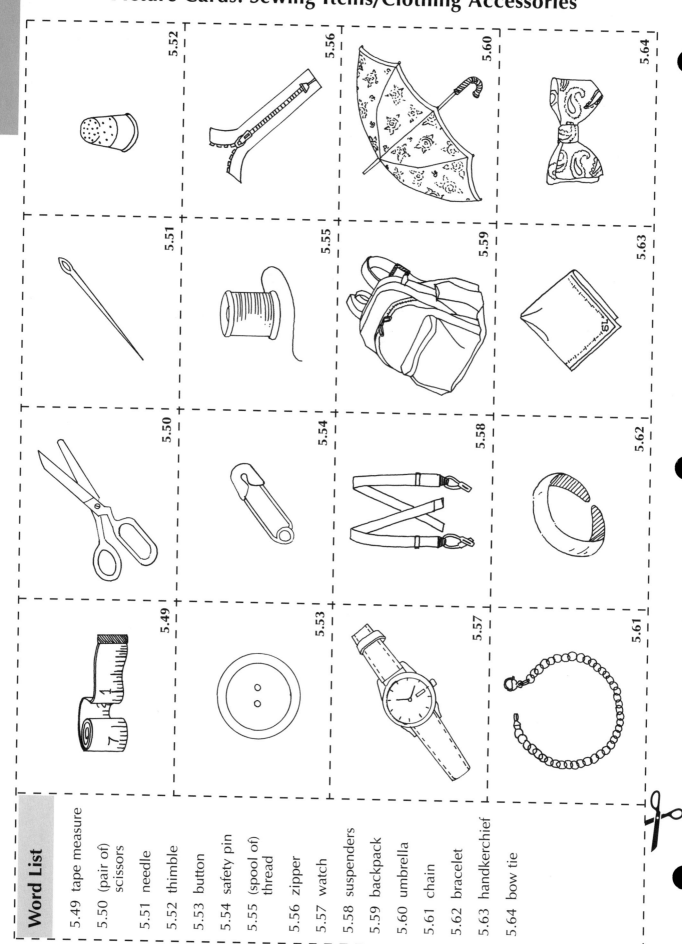

5.52

5.51

5.50

5.49

5.56

5.55

5.54

5.53

5.60

5.59

5.58

5.57

5.64

5.63

5.62

5.61

Page(s)	Activity	The Body (74–75)	Personal Hygiene (76–77)	Symptoms and Injuries (78)	Illnesses and Medical Conditions (79)	Health Care (80–81)	Medical Emergencies (82)	First Aid (83)	Clinics (84)	Medical and Dental Exams (85)	A Hospital (86–87)
86	**Body Language** (Round Table Label)	◆									
87	**You're the doctor!** (Survey)			◆	◆	◆		◆			
88–89	**What's happening at Wellnet?** (Information Exchange)				◆		◆	◆			
90–91	**Welby Community Clinic** (Picture Differences)								◆		◆
92	**The doctor will see you soon.** (Role Play)				◆	◆	◆	◆	◆	◆	◆
93	**Home Care or Hospital Care?** (Take a Stand)						◆	◆		◆	◆
94–95	**Health Board Game** (Board Game)	◆	◆	◆	◆	◆	◆	◆	◆	◆	◆
96–100	**Picture Card Activities and Picture Cards**	◆	◆	◆		◆		◆		◆	

Body Language

The The Oxford Picture Dictionary, pages 74–75. See page xii for Teacher's Notes.

◆ **Form groups of 4 people.**

◆ **Each person in the group takes turns labeling the parts of the body.**

◆ **After all the pictures have labels, look in the *Dictionary* to check your group's work.**

hand

◆ **What's next?** Take turns describing parts of the body to your group. *It's inside your mouth. It helps you talk.* (tongue) Have your classmates guess the answer.

86 Unit Six

You're the doctor!

The The Oxford Picture Dictionary, pages 78–81, 83. See page xiv for Teacher's Notes.

- ◆ Read the survey questions and mark your answers with a ✔.
- ◆ Ask and answer the questions again with nine classmates.
- ◆ Mark your classmates' answers on the survey form.

Would you rather...

		My Answers	My Classmates' Answers	No Opinion
...take throat lozenges or cough syrup for a cough?	a. throat lozenges			
	b. cough syrup			
...take cold tablets or vitamins for a cold?	a. cold tablets			
	b. vitamins			
...drink fluids or take antacids when you feel nauseous?	a. fluids			
	b. antacids			
...use a heating pad or an ice pack for a backache?	a. heating pad			
	b. ice pack			
...use nasal spray or a humidifier for nasal congestion?	a. nasal spray			
	b. humidifier			
...walk with crutches or a cane for a sprained ankle?	a. crutches			
	b. cane			

- ◆ **Complete the graph below. Chart only student preferences.**

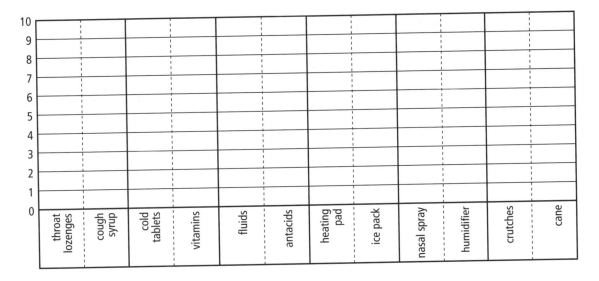

(Note: Your chart will not show the "No opinion" category.)

- ◆ **What's next?** Your teacher will ask you for your survey results. Write sentences about the answers. Follow the example below:

    Nine out of ten "doctors" in this class recommend cough syrup for a cough.

What's happening at Wellnet?

A

1

◆ Sit with a partner. (Don't show this paper to your partner!)

◆ Ask your partner about the missing information on the course schedule below.

◆ You can use these questions:

> *"What's the class?"*   *"What do you learn?"*   *"Where is it?"*   *"When is it?"*

◆ Write in the missing information and read it back to your partner to check your work.

WELLNET COMMUNITY HEALTH EDUCATION SCHEDULE OF CLASSES

CLASS	DESCRIPTION	LOCATION	TIME
First Aid	Instruction in CPR and rescue breathing.	Brod Clinic	Session 1: 6/7 Session 2: 6/14
Heimlich Maneuver	Emergency procedure for _____.	Gold Clinic Room A-4	Session 1: _____ _____ PM
Control	Make changes in diet and exercise.	Nayo Clinic	6/9 _____ PM
EMT Certification	Techniques for drug overdose, _____ , and _____ .	Children's Hospital/ West Wing Room 44	6/10: TBA _____ PM 6/24: 8–11 AM
Smoking and	New research: focus on teenagers.	Stein Clinic	One session: 7/16 6:30–9PM

2

◆ Use the immunization schedule below to answer your partner's questions.

WELLNET LOW-COST IMMUNIZATION SCHEDULE

VACCINE	AGE	LOCATION	COST
Flu shot	Seniors 55 and over Adults 21 and over	Shapiro Senior Center — Room 5 Nayo Clinic West	Free $15.00
Chicken pox	Infants 6 mo. 1 yr. – 5 yrs.	Children's Hospital Room B-3	$10.00
Measles, Mumps, & Rubella (MMR)	3–12 months 18 mos. – 3 yrs.	Children's Hospital Room A-9	$20.00
Tuberculosis (TB) screening	Children 6 and up Adults	Wellnet Mobile Clinic Same	$5.00 $7.00
Allergy shot *MD authorized	Adults 21 and over	Nayo Clinic East Room 4	$25.00

◆ **What's next?** Pretend you are planning a health education class for your neighborhood. What class would you offer? Work with a partner to make a flyer for the class.

What's happening at Wellnet?

The The Oxford Picture Dictionary, pages 79, 82–83. See page xviii for Teacher's Notes.

Information Exchange

B

- ◆ Sit with a partner. (Don't show this paper to your partner!)
- ◆ Use the course schedule below to answer your partner's questions.

WELLNET COMMUNITY HEALTH EDUCATION SCHEDULE OF CLASSES

CLASS	DESCRIPTION	LOCATION	TIME
First Aid	Instruction in CPR and rescue breathing.	Brod Clinic Room 12	Session 1: 6/7 Session 2: 6/14 9 AM – 12 PM
Heimlich Maneuver	Emergency procedure for choking.	Gold Clinic Room A-4	Session 1: 6/14 4 – 6 PM
Control Blood Pressure	Make changes in diet and exercise.	Nayo Clinic Auditorium A-1	6/9 7:30–9 PM
EMT Certification	Techniques for drug overdose, bleeding, and drowning.	Children's Hospital/ West Wing Room 44	6/10: TBA 6/17: 5–8 PM 6/24: 8–11 AM
Smoking and Cancer	New research: focus on teenagers.	Stein Clinic Room 15	One session: 7/16 6:30–9PM

- ◆ Ask your partner about the missing information on the immunization schedule below.
- ◆ You can use these questions:

    "What's the class?"   "What do you learn?"   "Where is it?"   "When is it?"

- ◆ Write in the missing information and read it back to your partner to check your work.

WELLNET LOW-COST IMMUNIZATION SCHEDULE

VACCINE	AGE	LOCATION	COST
Flu shot	Seniors 55 and over Adults 21 and over	Shapiro Senior Center — _____ Nayo Clinic West	Free _____
_____	Infants 6 mo. _____	Children's Hospital Room B-3	$10.00
Measles, _____, & Rubella (MMR)	_____ 18 mos. – 3 yrs.	Children's Hospital Room A-9	_____
Tuberculosis (TB) screening	_____ Adults	_____ Same	$5.00
_____shot *MD authorized	Adults 21 and over	Nayo Clinic East	_____

- ◆ **What's next?** Pretend you are planning a health education class for your neighborhood. What class would you offer? Work with a partner to make a flyer for the class.

Welby Community Clinic

The The Oxford Picture Dictionary, pages 84, 86–87. See page xvi for Teacher's Notes.

Picture Differences

A

◆ **Sit with a partner and look at each other's papers.**
◆ **There are 10 differences between your pictures.**
◆ **Work with your partner to find the differences.**

◆ **Write the differerences you find on the chart below.**

A	B
1. receptionist is sitting	receptionist is standing
2.	
3.	
4.	
5.	
6.	
7.	
8.	
9.	
10.	

◆ **What's next?** Your teacher will bring in the yellow pages. Find advertisements for health clinics. List their services and ask questions with your partner:

    When is it open?   *Can you use an insurance card?*   *What does the clinic do?*

Welby Community Clinic

- ◆ **Sit with a partner and look at each other's papers.**
- ◆ **There are 10 differences between your pictures.**
- ◆ **Work with your partner to find the differences.**

- ◆ **Write the differerences you find on the chart below.**

A	B
1. receptionist is sitting	receptionist is standing
2.	
3.	
4.	
5.	
6.	
7.	
8.	
9.	
10.	

- ◆ **What's next?** Your teacher will bring in the yellow pages. Find advertisements for health clinics. List their services and ask questions with your partner:

  When is it open?   *Can you use an insurance card?*   *What does the clinic do?*

The doctor will see you soon.

The The Oxford Picture Dictionary, pages 79–87. See page xix for Teacher's Notes.

Role Play

- ◆ **Form groups of 4 people.**
- ◆ **Practice saying all the lines.**
- ◆ **Choose your character and decide what you will say.**
- ◆ **Think of other things your character can say.**
- ◆ **Act out your role play.**

THE CHARACTERS:

two patients
a receptionist
a nurse

THE SCENE:

An urgent care clinic where walk-in patients need immediate medical care. A receptionist asks for and gives information. The nurse sees patients in the exam room.

THE PROPS:

a clipboard
an insurance card
a health form

THE SCRIPT:

Who says...	...these lines?
a receptionist	I need a copy of your insurance card*.
	Please help me! I burned myself!
	What's that? Will it hurt?
	Oh, that's a stethoscope. We use it to listen to your heart.
	No, there's no history of diabetes in my family.
	See the nurse first. She is going to draw blood.
	The doctor says you need stitches on that leg.
	Excuse me. Where do I pick up my prescription medicine?
	Sorry. There's no smoking in the waiting room.
	I'll put your walker next to the examination table.
	You'll have to wait to see the pediatrician.
	Here's some information about measles.
	Do you have any other questions?

* You can substitute other vocabulary for the underlined words.

- ◆ **What's next?** Look at page 82 in your *Dictionary*. Discuss what you should do in these emergency situations. Your teacher will write your ideas on the board.

Home Care or Hospital Care?

Take a Stand

◆ **Think about the reasons to choose home care or hospital care.**

◆ **Read each statement on the list.**

◆ **If the statement shows that <u>home care</u> is a good idea, make a ✓ in that column.**

◆ **If the statement shows that <u>hospital care</u> is a good idea, make a ✓ in that column.**

◆ **For K and L, think of two more statements to add to this list.**

STATEMENTS	home care	hospital care
A. Hospital staff is available 24 hours, day and night.		
B. Registered nurses can do blood work at a patient's home.		
C. Nurse midwives charge less than a gynecologist for home births.		
D. Some hospital volunteers can translate different languages.		
E. Most people don't sleep well in hospital beds.		
F. Dieticians plan healthy meals for patients.		
G. Medical insurance doesn't pay for many home care expenses.		
H. Family members can learn CPR and first aid treatments.		
I. Some elderly people can overdose on drugs by accident.		
J. Few doctors make house calls anymore.		
K.		
L.		

◆ **Sit with a partner and compare papers.**

◆ **Write your and your partner's ideas.**

I think _____ *care is better because* _____
_____.

My partner thinks _____ *care is better because* _____
_____.

◆ **What's next?** What medical problems are best treated at home? What medical problems are best treated in a hospital? Your teacher will write your ideas on the board.

Health Board.

tape here

Draw
something in your medicine cabinet. Describe it.

Name
something you see in a medical clinic.

Pick a health card. Say 3 things about it.

Answer:
What kind of soap do you use?

In 15 seconds...
name 3 different things in a hospital.

To begin...
- Put your markers on start.
- Take turns flipping a coin to move your marker around the board.

moves one space

moves two spaces

- Follow the directions on the squares.
- Ask your group for help when you don't know the answer.

Act out
a symptom or injury for your group. (The group has to guess what it is!)

Finish

Start

Pick a health card.

Spell it.

Name
a product you use on your face.

tape here

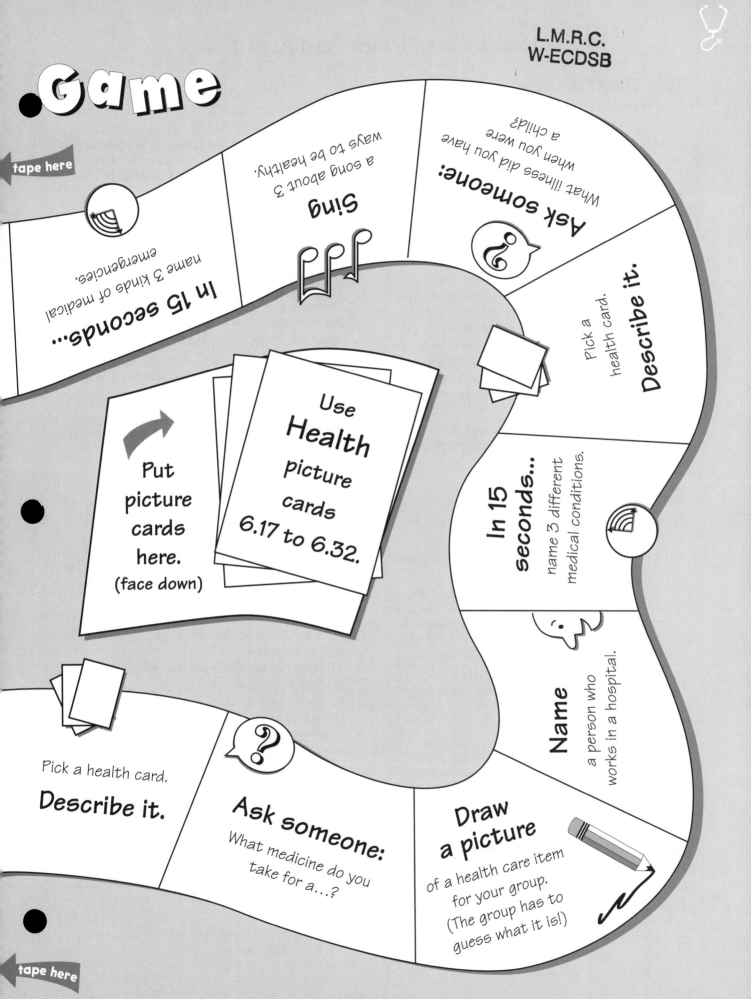

Health Care Picture Card Activities

PEER DICTATION (Pairs)

Parts of the Body Picture Cards, page 97

1. Duplicate a class set of the picture card pages and cut off the Word List on the sidebar. (Hold on to these for step 6.)

2. Pair students and give student A the picture card page.

3. Direct the B students to look at page 74 in the *Dictionary* and read off the names of the body parts. When the A students hear a body part that is on their picture page, they say *I have that. How do you spell it?* B students spell out the word so that the A's can write it under the picture.

4. When the A's have written all the body parts words, they put their papers aside. B's then get a picture card page and listen to A's read the list from page 75. They request the spelling of the body parts and write them under the pictures on their pages.

5. Once the B's have finished, have the A's close their dictionaries. Partners can then work together to label their respective pages.

6. As a final check for accuracy, hand out the Word Lists you put aside in step 1 so that students can check their spelling.

MIXER (Whole Class)

Symptoms and Injuries/Health Care Picture Cards, page 98

1. Duplicate enough copies of the picture card page so that each student can have one card.

2. Give half of the students a symptoms and injury card. These students are "patients." Give the other half a health care picture card. These students are "pharmacists." Have all the "patients" go to one side of the room and all the "pharmacists" go to the other.

3. Have patients go up to the pharmacists to find a remedy.
   -*I have a headache. Can you help me?*
   -*Yes. I recommend pain reliever.*
   - *I'm sorry. I don't have what you need. I only have nasal spray.*

4. The activity ends when everyone finds a correct match.

NOW AND THEN CHARADES (Groups)

Health and Personal Hygiene Verbs Picture Cards, page 99

1. Duplicate one picture card page for each group of 4-5 students.

2. Give each group one picture card page. Tell students to number off. Have #1 cut apart the picture cards. Have #2 shuffle the cards and place them

face down on a desk. Identify #4 as the recorder.

3. For the first round, Student #1 picks a card from the deck, asks *What am I doing?* and pantomimes the action until the group can name it. Once the group names the action, *You're making an appointment,* student #1 sits down.

4. The recorder then asks the group, *What did Carlos do?* Group members reach consensus on the correct way to put the sentence in the past, using the **Verb Guide** on pages 170–172 in the *Dictionary* to check the correct past tense form. The recorder writes the group's response on a sheet of paper for example, *Carlos made an appointment.*

5. Student #2 picks a card and the activity continues.

6. The activity is over when all the students in the group have had two turns. Recorders can read from or turn in their papers.

TWIN GRIDS (Pairs)

Personal Hygiene/Health Care Picture Cards, page 100
Grid, page 197

1. Duplicate one copy of the grid on page 197 and number each square 1-16 to create a large discount drugstore with "aisles" to indicate where various products are located. Give each student one grid and one picture card page. (If you have an overhead projector, see Using the Overhead Projector in the Picture Cards Teacher's Notes, page x.)

2. Have students cut apart their picture cards and place them face up and spread out, on their desks next to the grid.

3. Tell students to put the soap in aisle #4. Direct students to place the picture of soap on grid square #4. Encourage students to ask clarification questions. *Did you say soap? Put it in aisle 4 or 14?, etc.*

4. Continue telling students where to put all the items until all the grid squares are filled. Have students compare their grids with one another as you clarify any discrepancies.

5. Next pair students. Give each pair a manila folder to use as a screen between the partners. Have one partner (the manager) tell the other (stock clerk) *Put the soap in aisle 7.* (Students do not have to use the same sentences you used.) Both partners place their pictures on the grids. When the grids are complete, senders and receivers compare their grids.

6. Have the senders (managers) and the receivers (clerks) switch roles.

Picture Cards: Parts of the Body

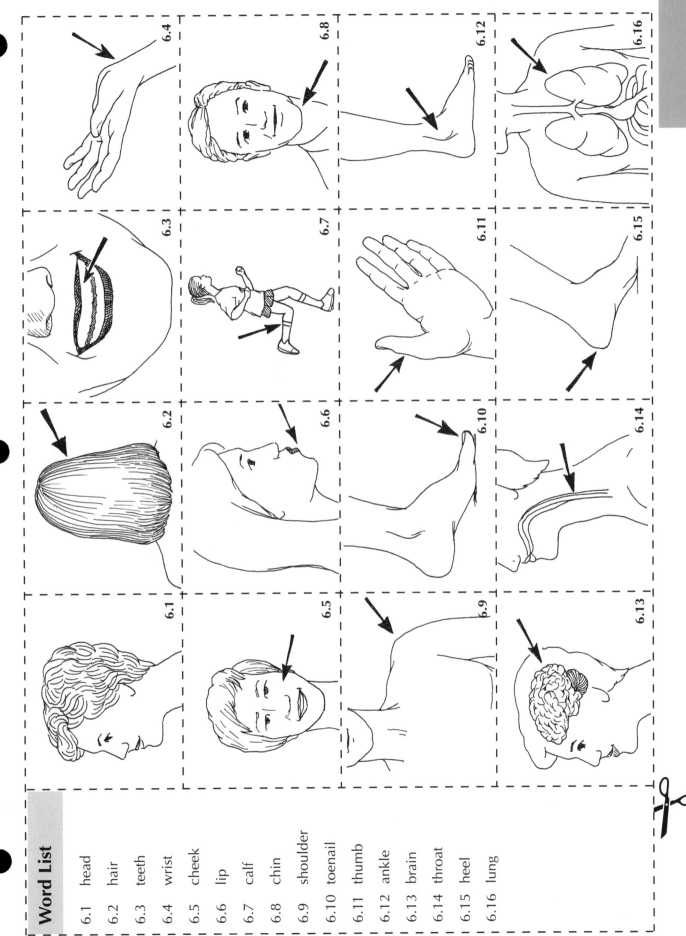

Word List	
6.1	head
6.2	hair
6.3	teeth
6.4	wrist
6.5	cheek
6.6	lip
6.7	calf
6.8	chin
6.9	shoulder
6.10	toenail
6.11	thumb
6.12	ankle
6.13	brain
6.14	throat
6.15	heel
6.16	lung

Picture Cards: Symptoms and Injuries/Health Care

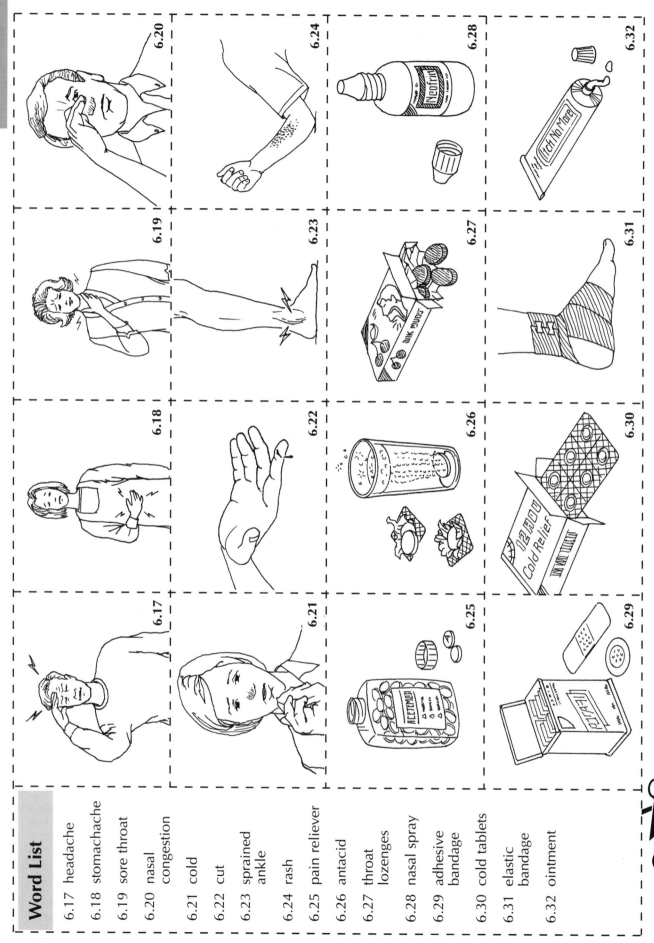

Word List

6.17 headache
6.18 stomachache
6.19 sore throat
6.20 nasal congestion
6.21 cold
6.22 cut
6.23 sprained ankle
6.24 rash
6.25 pain reliever
6.26 antacid
6.27 throat lozenges
6.28 nasal spray
6.29 adhesive bandage
6.30 cold tablets
6.31 elastic bandage
6.32 ointment

Picture Cards: Health and Personal Hygiene Verbs

Picture Cards: Personal Hygiene/Health Care

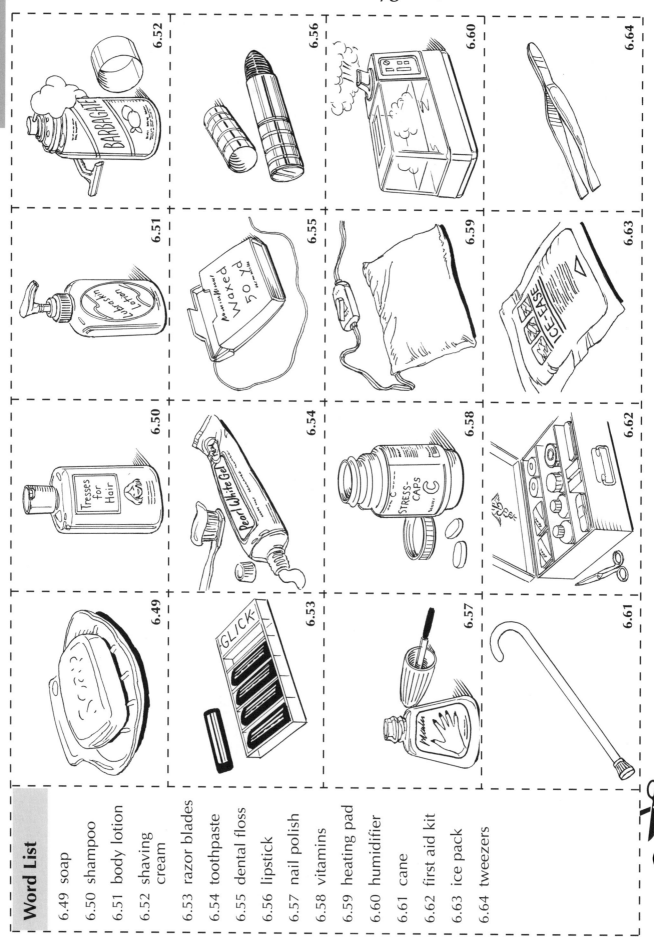

6.52

6.56

6.60

6.64

6.51

6.55

6.59

6.63

6.50

6.54

6.58

6.62

6.49

6.53

6.57

6.61

7. Community

Page(s)	Activity	City Streets (88–89)	An Intersection (90–91)	A Mall (92–93)	A Childcare Center (94–95)	U.S. Mail (96)	A Bank (97)	A Library (98)	The Legal System (99)	Crime (100)	Public Safety (101)	Emergencies and Natural Disasters (102–103)
102	**Around the Corner** (Round Table Label)		◆									
103	**Around Town** (Mixer)	◆				◆	◆	◆				
104–105	**Paradise Hills Mall** (Picture Differences)			◆								
106–107	**Worldwide Disasters** (Information Exchange)											◆
108	**Order in the court!** (Role Play)								◆	◆		
109	**Sidewalk Vendors –Yes or No?** (Take a Stand)		◆									
110–111	**Community Board Game** (Board Game)	◆	◆	◆	◆	◆	◆	◆	◆	◆	◆	◆
112–116	**Picture Card Activities and Picture Cards**	◆	◆		◆	◆	◆	◆				

Around the Corner

The Oxford Picture Dictionary, pages 90–91, 96. See page xii for Teacher's Notes.

- ◆ Form groups of 4 people.
- ◆ Each person in the group takes turns labeling the items on this paper.
- ◆ After all the pictures have labels, look in the *Dictionary* to check your group's work.

- ◆ **What's next?** What's around the corner from your home? Draw a picture and label the people, places, and things that you see. Talk about your picture with the class.

Around Town

The Oxford Picture Dictionary, pages 88–89, 96–98. See page xiii for Teacher's Notes.

Mixer

- ◆ **Write the missing letters in the words.**
- ◆ **Walk around the room. Ask and answer the questions.**
- ◆ **Write a different name in each box.**

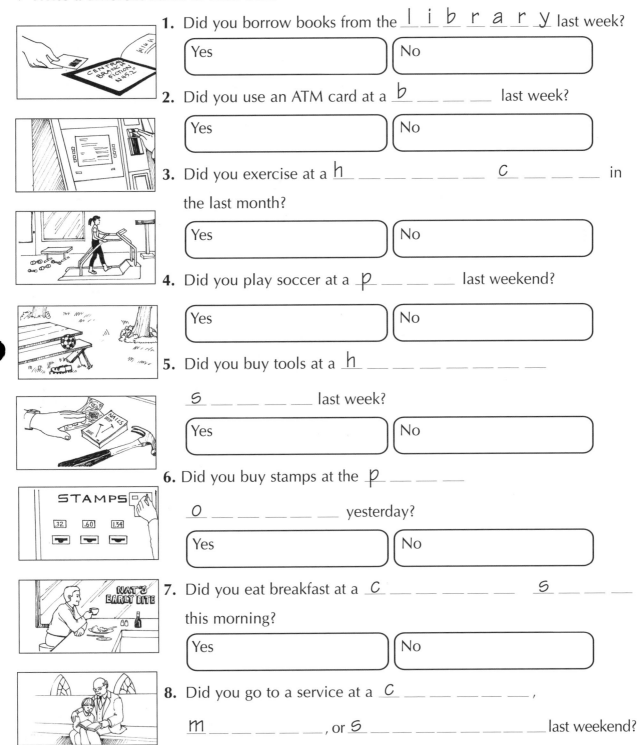

1. Did you borrow books from the l i b r a r y last week?

Yes	No

2. Did you use an ATM card at a b ___ ___ ___ last week?

Yes	No

3. Did you exercise at a h ___ ___ ___ ___ ___ c ___ ___ ___ in the last month?

Yes	No

4. Did you play soccer at a p ___ ___ ___ last weekend?

Yes	No

5. Did you buy tools at a h ___ ___ ___ ___ ___ ___ ___ s ___ ___ ___ ___ ___ last week?

Yes	No

6. Did you buy stamps at the p ___ ___ ___ o ___ ___ ___ ___ ___ yesterday?

Yes	No

7. Did you eat breakfast at a c ___ ___ ___ ___ ___ ___ s ___ ___ ___ this morning?

Yes	No

8. Did you go to a service at a c ___ ___ ___ ___ ___ , m ___ ___ ___ ___ ___ ___ , or s ___ ___ ___ ___ ___ ___ ___ last weekend?

Yes	No

- ◆ **What's next?** Think about the types of places in your neighborhood now and in the neighborhood where you lived before. Make a list comparing both places and share it with a partner.

Paradise Hills Mall

The Oxford Picture Dictionary, pages 92–93. See page xvi for Teacher's Notes.

A

Picture Differences

- ◆ **Sit with a partner and look at each other's papers.**
- ◆ **There are 10 differences between your pictures.**
- ◆ **Work with your partner to find the differences.**

- ◆ **Write the differences you find on the chart below.**

A	B
1. music store on 1st floor	music store on 2nd floor
2.	
3.	
4.	
5.	
6.	
7.	
8.	
9.	
10.	

104 Unit Seven

Paradise Hills Mall

The Oxford Picture Dictionary, pages 92–93. See page xvi for Teacher's Notes.

- ◆ Sit with a partner and look at each other's papers.
- ◆ There are 10 differences between your pictures.
- ◆ Work with your partner to find the differences.

- ◆ Write the differences you find on the chart below.

A	B
1. music store on 1st floor	music store on 2nd floor
2.	
3.	
4.	
5.	
6.	
7.	
8.	
9.	
10.	

Worldwide Disasters

The Oxford Picture Dictionary, pages 102–103. See page xviii for Teacher's Notes.

Information Exchange

A

1

- ◆ Sit with a partner. (Don't show this paper to your partner!)
- ◆ Ask your partner about the missing information in the headlines below.
- ◆ You can use these questions:

    "When was the _____ ?"   *"Where was the _____ ?"*

    "What happened in _____ ?"   *"What did the _____ do?"*

- ◆ Write in the missing information and read it back to your partner to check your work.

AROUND THE GLOBE

January_____, _____

7.2 Earthquake Hits Japan!

Kobe, Kyoto, Osaka Hit
$100 billion damage
Thousands homeless

Newswatch Magazine

_____ 21, _____

Terrorist Bomb Explodes
over Lockerbie, Scotland
_____ on board Pan-Am 747
and 11 on ground killed

International Times

April 26, _____

Explosion in Chernobyl

_____ , _____

Nuclear Power Plant
_____ spread
throughout Eastern
and Western Europe

U.S. WEEKLY

August 22-26, 1992

★★★★★

**Most Costly Hurricane
in U.S. History!**

"Andrew" hits_____,
Louisiana, and Bahamas
$20.6 billion damage

2

- ◆ Use the headlines below to answer your partner's questions.

THE DAILY JOURNAL

March 25, 1911

Fire and Riot in New York City!
TRIANGLE SHIRTWAIST FACTORY BURNS
145 women workers die

Washington Report

1935-1936

Drought Continues!
Arkansas, Oklahoma, and Texas Worst Areas
Dust covers 50 million acres

The Gazette May 31, 1889

FLOOD OVER JOHNSTOWN!
Pennsylvania City Destroyed
2,200 People Dead
Homes and businesses washed away

Atlantic Post

March 11-14, 1888
Blizzard Buries 400
New York, New Jersey, Massachusetts covered in 5 feet of snow
$20 MILLION IN DAMAGES

- ◆ **What's next?** Choose one of the disasters or emergencies. Work with your partner to think of ways to prevent or survive the disaster. Share your ideas with the class.

Worldwide Disasters

The Oxford Picture Dictionary, pages 102–103. See page xviii for Teacher's Notes.

1

- ◆ Sit with a partner. (Don't show this paper to your partner!)
- ◆ Use the headlines below to answer your partner's questions.

AROUND THE GLOBE

January 17, 1995

7.2 Earthquake Hits Japan!

Kobe, Kyoto, Osaka Hit
$100 billion damage
Thousands homeless

Newswatch Magazine

December 21, 1988

AIRPLANE CRASH

Terrorist Bomb Explodes
over Lockerbie, Scotland
259 on board Pan-Am 747
and 11 on ground killed

International Times

April 26, 1986

Explosion in Chernobyl Kiev, U.S.S.R.

Nuclear Power Plant
Radiation spread
throughout Eastern
and Western Europe

U.S. WEEKLY

August 22-26, 1992

★★★★★

Most Costly Hurricane in U.S. History!

"Andrew" hits Florida,
Louisiana, and Bahamas
$20.6 billion damage

2

- ◆ Ask your partner about the missing information in the headlines below.
- ◆ You can use these questions:

  "When was the _____ ?"   *"Where was the _____ ?"*

  "What happened in _____ ?"   *"What did the _____ do?"*

- ◆ Write in the missing information and read it back to your partner to check your work.

THE DAILY JOURNAL
——— March 25, 1911 ———
_____ and Riot in New York City!
TRIANGLE SHIRTWAIST _____
145 women workers die

The Gazette May__, __
FLOOD OVER JOHNSTOWN!
Pennsylvania City Destroyed
_____
Homes and businesses washed away

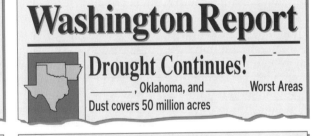

Washington Report
Drought Continues!
_____, Oklahoma, and _____ Worst Areas
Dust covers 50 million acres

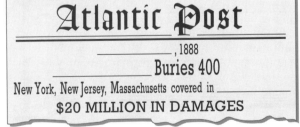

Atlantic Post
_____, 1888
_____ Buries 400
New York, New Jersey, Massachusetts covered in _____
$20 MILLION IN DAMAGES

- ◆ **What's next?** Choose one of the disasters or emergencies. Work with your partner to think of ways to prevent or survive the disaster. Share your ideas with the class.

Order in the court!

The Oxford Picture Dictionary, pages 99–100. See page xix for Teacher's Notes.

Role Play

- ◆ **Form groups of 4 people.**
- ◆ **Practice saying all the lines.**
- ◆ **Choose your character and decide what you will say.**
- ◆ **Think of other things your character can say.**
- ◆ **Act out your role play.**

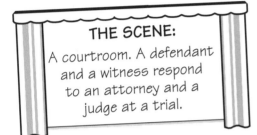

THE SCENE:
A courtroom. A defendant and a witness respond to an attorney and a judge at a trial.

THE CHARACTERS:
a judge
an attorney
a defendant
a witness

THE PROPS:
a pen
a legal pad
selected clothing or accessory items used as "evidence"

THE SCRIPT:

Who says...	...these lines?
a judge	Could you please state your <u>name</u>* for the court?
	I'm sure that's <u>him</u>. <u>He</u> was wearing <u>a baseball cap</u>.
	Where were you on the night of <u>September 15th</u>?
	I was working at <u>Friendly Freeze</u>. I worked until <u>10:00 p.m.</u>
	I think <u>he</u> had a <u>gun</u>. I saw it in <u>his jacket</u>.
	Will the <u>prosecuting attorney</u> please come forward?
	Your honor, may I show this <u>picture</u> to the court?
	That's not my <u>baseball cap</u>. It's too <u>small</u>.
	If you are <u>guilty</u>, the jail sentence is <u>60 days</u>.
	What was the suspect wearing during the <u>robbery</u>?
	He was wearing <u>black pants</u> and <u>a blue shirt</u>.
	I can prove I'm innocent. Ask my <u>boss</u>.

* You can substitute other vocabulary for the underlined words.

- ◆ **What's next?** Invite one group to come to the front and present their trial. This group will leave the room for two minutes while the classroom "jury members" discuss the case and decide on a verdict.

Sidewalk Vendors — Yes or No?

The Oxford Picture Dictionary, pages 90–91. See page xx for Teacher's Notes.   **Take a Stand**

- ◆ **Think about the reasons to buy from a sidewalk vendor.**
- ◆ **Read each statement on the list.**
- ◆ **If the statement shows that buying from a sidewalk vendor is <u>a good idea</u>, make a ✓ in that column.**
- ◆ **If the statement shows that buying from a sidewalk vendor is <u>not a good idea</u>, make a ✓ in that column.**
- ◆ **For K and L, think of two more statements to add to this list.**

STATEMENTS	+	−
A. Sidewalk vendors usually don't charge sales tax.		
B. Vendors don't have space for different kinds of items.		
C. People enjoy selling food or clothes they make themselves.		
D. Sidewalk vendors usually know the people in the neighborhood.		
E. Exchanging things or returning them to a sidewalk vendor is difficult.		
F. It's fun to try to get a better deal by offering a lower price.		
G. Many vendors don't have a license to sell things.		
H. Sidewalk vendors move around from corner to corner.		
I. You usually can't pay with a check or credit card.		
J. Farms sell fruits and vegetables directly to sidewalk vendors.		
K.		
L.		

- ◆ **Sit with a partner and compare papers.**
- ◆ **Write your and your partner's ideas.**

I think buying from sidewalk vendors is a _____ *because* _____

_____ .

My partner thinks buying from sidewalk vendors is a _____ *because*

_____ .

- ◆ **What's next?** Take a stand. Your teacher will tell you where to stand if you support street vendors and where to stand if you don't support street vendors.

Unit Seven 109

Community Board

Draw a place in your neighborhood. Describe it.

Name a crime that you think is a problem in your community.

Pick a community card. Say 3 things about it.

Answer: What emergency information do you keep in your wallet?

In 15 seconds... name 5 different things you see in a library.

To begin...

- Put your markers on start.
- Take turns flipping a coin to move your marker around the board.

 moves one space

 moves two spaces

- Follow the directions on the squares.
- Ask your group for help when you don't know the answer.

Act out something you do with children. (The group has to guess what it is!)

Finish

Start

Pick a community card. **Spell it.**

Name
a store in your neighborhood and say what you buy there.

Game

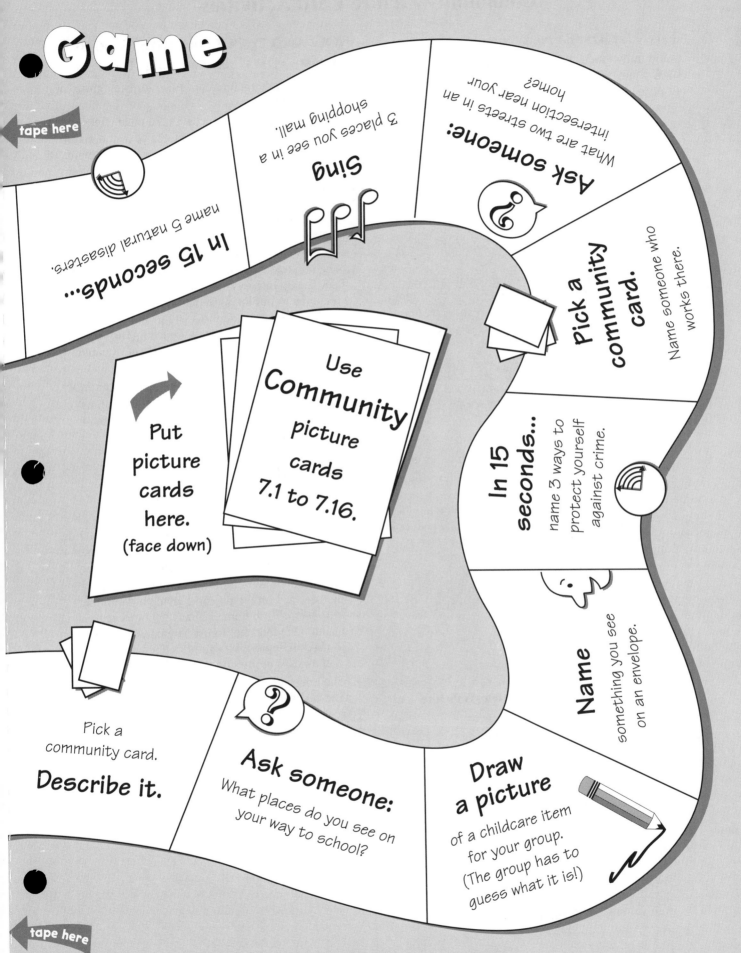

tape here

name 5 natural disasters.

In 15 seconds...

Sing

3 places you see in a shopping mall.

Ask someone:
What are two streets in an intersection near your home?

Pick a community card.

Name someone who works there.

Use Community picture cards 7.1 to 7.16.

Put picture cards here. (face down)

In 15 seconds...
name 3 ways to protect yourself against crime.

Name something you see on an envelope.

Pick a community card.
Describe it.

Ask someone:
What places do you see on your way to school?

Draw a picture of a childcare item for your group. (The group has to guess what it is!)

tape here

Community Picture Card Activities

TWIN GRIDS (Pairs)

Community Places Picture Cards, page 113
Grid, page 197

1. Duplicate one copy of the grid on page 197. Write letters A-D horizontally above the top 4 squares, and numbers 1-4 vertically next to the squares on the left side. Give each student one grid and one picture card page. (If you have an overhead projector, see Using the Overhead Projector in the Picture Card Teacher's Notes, page x.)

2. Have students cut apart their picture cards and place them face up and spread out on their desks next to the grid.

3. Tell students that letters A-D represent avenues and numbers 1-4 represent streets. Practice identifying intersections: Find *Avenue A* and *1st Street.* Tell students that the post office is located on the corner of Avenue B and 1st Street. Direct students to place the post office picture on the grid square that corresponds to Avenue B and 1st Street. Encourage students to ask clarification questions. *Did you say post office? 1st or 3rd Street? Was that Avenue B or C?* etc.

4. Continue telling students where to put what until all the grid squares are filled. Have students compare their grids with one another as you clarify any discrepancies.

5. Next pair students. Give each pair a manila folder to use as a screen between the partners. Have one partner (the sender) tell the other (the receiver) *Put the post office on Avenue B and 1st Street.* [Students do not have to copy your sentences.] Both partners place their pictures on the grids. When the grids are complete, senders and receivers compare their grids.

6. Have senders and receivers switch roles.

PICK A PAIR (Pairs)

Community People/Community Items A Picture Cards, page 114

1. Pair students and give each pair one picture card page.

2. Have the pair cut up the cards, shuffle them and place them face down in four rows of four cards.

3. Have partners take turns turning over two cards at a time, trying to match community people with related items. When the cards match, for example, *letter carrier/package*, the student keeps the cards if she can make a sentence: *The letter carrier delivers a package.* If the student can't make the sentence or the cards don't match, (for example, *letter carrier/fire hydrant*), the student turns the cards back over.

4. The activity ends when all the cards are gone.

NOW AND THEN CHARADES (Groups)

Community Verbs Picture Cards, page 115

1. Duplicate one picture card page for each group of 4-5 students.

2. Give each group one picture card page. Tell students to number off. Have #1 cut apart the picture cards. Have #2 shuffle the cards and place them face down on a desk. Identify #4 as the recorder.

3. For the first round, Student #1 picks a card from the deck, asks *What am I doing?,* and pantomimes the action until the group can name it. Once the group names the action, for example, *You're pushing a stroller,* student #1 sits down.

4. The recorder then asks the group: *What did Carlos do?* Group members reach consensus on the correct way to put the sentence in the past, using the **Verb Guide** on pages 170–172 in the *Dictionary* to check the correct past tense form. The recorder writes the group's response on a sheet of paper. *Carlos pushed the stroller.*

5. Student #2 picks a card and the activity continues.

6. The activity is over when all the students in the group have had two turns. Recorders can read from or turn in their papers.

GUESS WHAT? (Groups)

Community Items B Picture Cards, page 116

1. Have students form small groups of 2-4 students.

2. Give each group one page of cut-up picture cards. Have one student in the group shuffle the cards and place them face down on the table.

3. Each student takes a turn picking up the top picture card on the pile and giving a definition. *You need this to borrow a book.* (library card) Caution students not to use any part of the word in their definition; for example, they can't say, *You use this at the library.* (library card)

4. The other group members try to guess the word. The first student to guess the word keeps the picture card.

5. The activity ends when all the cards are guessed correctly.

Picture Cards: Community Places

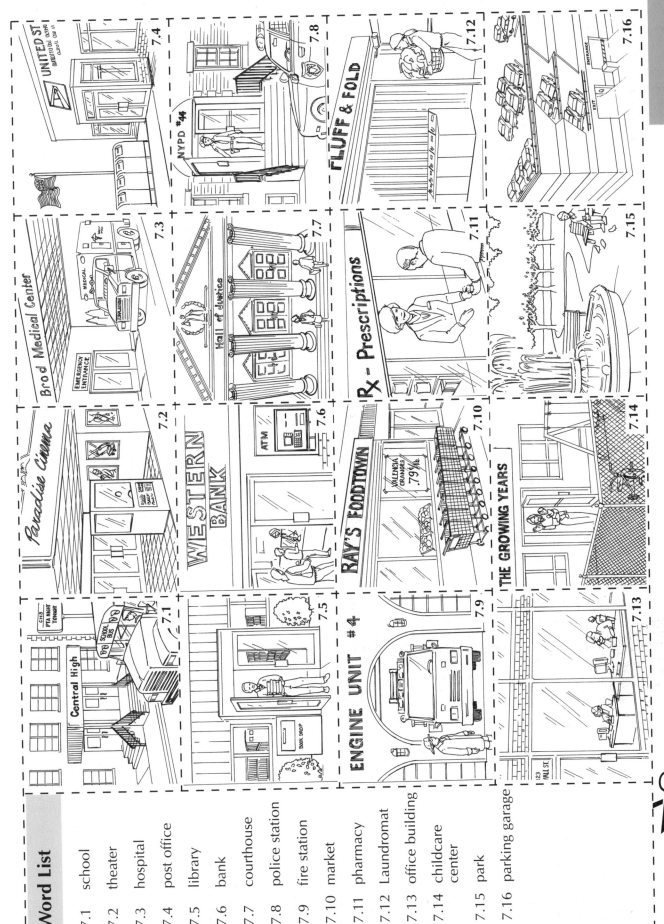

7.4 UNITED ST
7.8 NYPD #44
7.12 FLUFF & FOLD
7.16 ENTRANCE / EXIT

7.3 Brod Medical Center / EMERGENCY ENTRANCE / MEDICAL
7.7 Hall of Justice
7.11 Rx – Prescriptions
7.15

7.2 Paradise Cinema
7.6 WESTERN BANK / ATM
7.10 RAY'S FOODTOWN / VALENCIA ORANGES .79¢/lb.
7.14 THE GROWING YEARS

7.1 Central High / PTA NIGHT TONIGHT / SCHOOL BUS
7.5 BOOK DROP
7.9 ENGINE UNIT #4
7.13 123 MALL ST.

Word List

7.1	school
7.2	theater
7.3	hospital
7.4	post office
7.5	library
7.6	bank
7.7	courthouse
7.8	police station
7.9	fire station
7.10	market
7.11	pharmacy
7.12	Laundromat
7.13	office building
7.14	childcare center
7.15	park
7.16	parking garage

Picture Cards: Community People/Community Items A

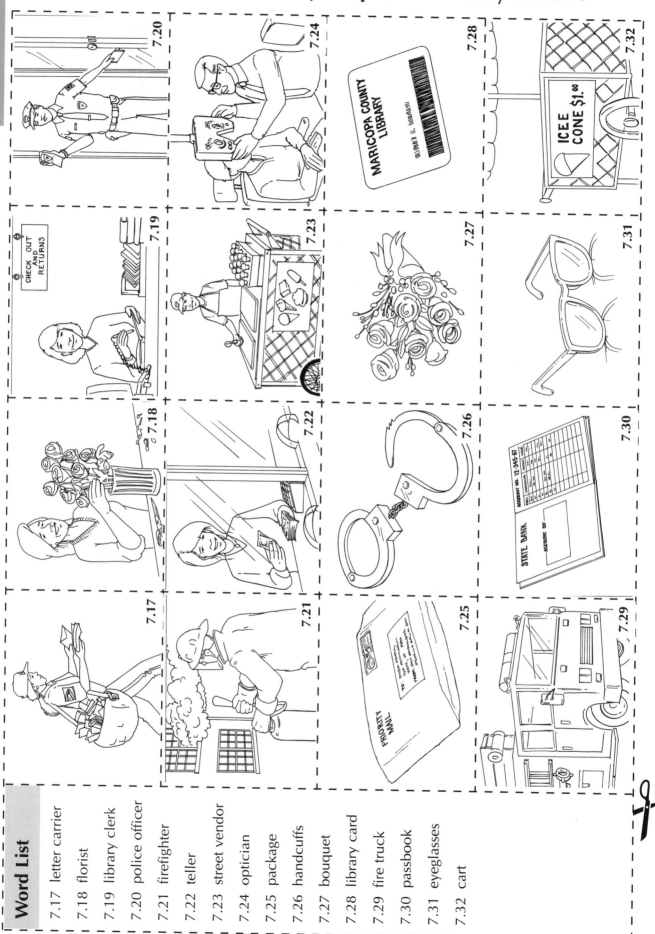

© 1999 Oxford University Press   Permission granted to reproduce for classroom use.

Word List

7.17 letter carrier
7.18 florist
7.19 library clerk
7.20 police officer
7.21 firefighter
7.22 teller
7.23 street vendor
7.24 optician
7.25 package
7.26 handcuffs
7.27 bouquet
7.28 library card
7.29 fire truck
7.30 passbook
7.31 eyeglasses
7.32 cart

Picture Cards: Community Verbs

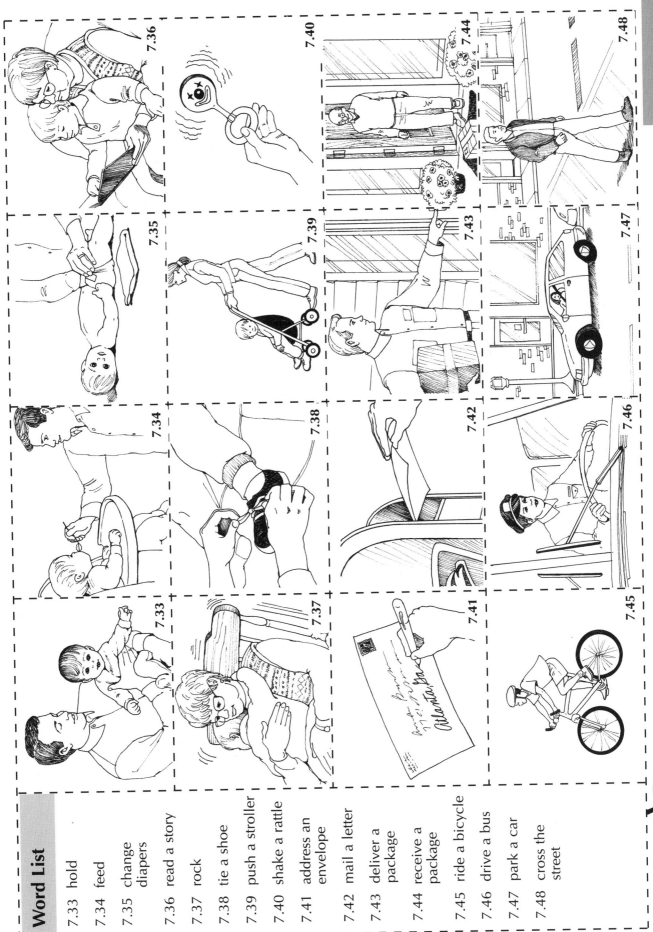

Word List	
7.33	hold
7.34	feed
7.35	change diapers
7.36	read a story
7.37	rock
7.38	tie a shoe
7.39	push a stroller
7.40	shake a rattle
7.41	address an envelope
7.42	mail a letter
7.43	deliver a package
7.44	receive a package
7.45	ride a bicycle
7.46	drive a bus
7.47	park a car
7.48	cross the street

Picture Cards: Community Items B

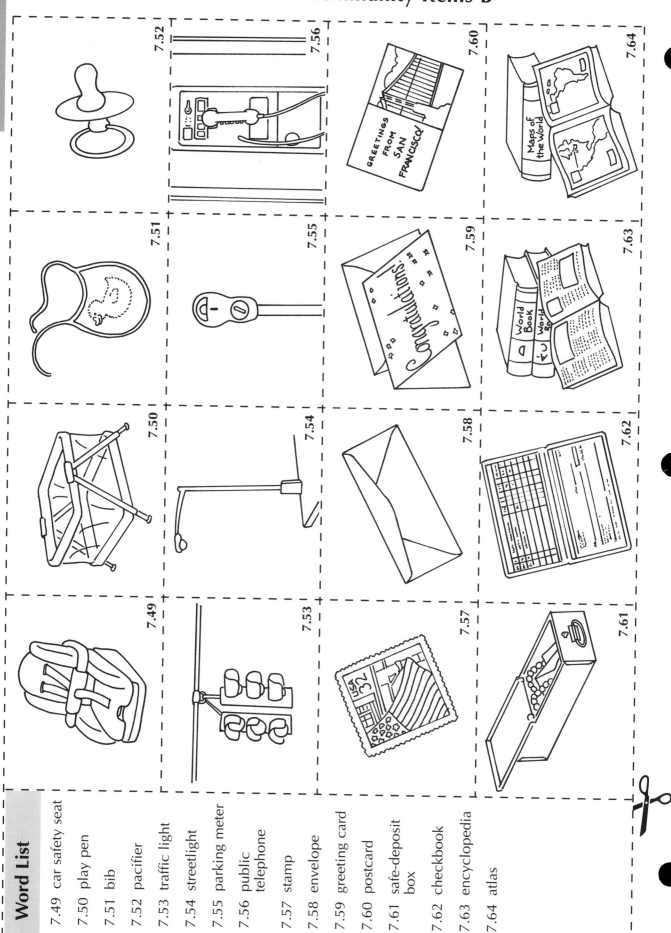

7.52

7.56

7.60

7.64

7.51

7.55

7.59

7.63

7.50

7.54

7.58

7.62

7.49

7.53

7.57

7.61

Word List

7.49 car safety seat
7.50 play pen
7.51 bib
7.52 pacifier
7.53 traffic light
7.54 streetlight
7.55 parking meter
7.56 public telephone
7.57 stamp
7.58 envelope
7.59 greeting card
7.60 postcard
7.61 safe-deposit box
7.62 checkbook
7.63 encyclopedia
7.64 atlas

8. Transportation

Page(s)		Public Transportation (104)	Prepositions of Motion (105)	Cars and Trucks (106)	Directions and Traffic Signs (107)	Parts of a Car and Car Maintenance (108–109)	An Airport (110)	A Plane Trip (111)
118	**Traveling on Route 66** (Round Table Label)	◆	◆	◆				
119	**What's the best way to travel?** (Survey)	◆		◆				
120–121	**Fly Skyair** (Picture Differences)		◆				◆	◆
122–123	**Destination San Francisco!** (Information Exchange)	◆		◆				
124	**The Friendly Skies** (Role Play)						◆	◆
125	**Drive a Car or Take Public Transportation?** (Take a Stand)	◆		◆				
126–127	**Transportation Board Game** (Board Game)	◆	◆	◆	◆	◆	◆	◆
128–132	**Picture Card Activities and Picture Cards**	◆		◆	◆	◆		

Traveling on Route 66

The Oxford Picture Dictionary, pages 104–105, 106. See page xii for Teacher's Notes.

Round Table Label

♦ **Form groups of 4 people.**

♦ **Each person in the group takes turns labeling the items on this paper.**

♦ **After all the pictures have labels, look in the *Dictionary* to check your group's work.**

♦ **What's next?** What public transportation do you have in your area? Make a list with your group and discuss each one. Use these questions: How much is the fare? Is it safe? Is it fast? Is the schedule convenient? Where do you go?

What's the best way to travel?

The Oxford Picture Dictionary, pages 104–106. See page xiv for Teacher's Notes.

- ◆ **Read the survey questions and mark your answers.**
- ◆ **Ask and answer the questions again with nine classmates.**
- ◆ **Mark your classmates' answers on the survey form.**

Do you prefer...

		My Answers	My Classmates' Answers	No Opinion
...a plane or a train?	a. plane			
	b. train			
...a sports car or a station wagon?	a. sports car			
	b. station wagon			
...a bus or a subway?	a. bus			
	b. subway			
...a pickup truck or a convertible?	a. pickup truck			
	b. convertible			
...a minivan or a full-size car?	a. minivan			
	b. full-size car			
...a sports utility vehicle or a motorcycle?	a. sports utility vehicle			
	b. motorcycle			

- ◆ **Complete the graph below. Chart only student preferences.**

a   b   (Note: Your chart will not show the "No opinion" category.)

10											
9											
8											
7											
6											
5											
4											
3											
2											
1											
0	plane	train	sports car	station wagon	bus	subway	pickup truck	convertible	minivan	full-size car	SUV	motorcycle

- ◆ **What's next?** Your teacher will ask you for your survey results. Write sentences about the answers. Follow the example below:

    Fewer students prefer traveling by plane.

Fly Skyair

The Oxford Picture Dictionary, pages 105, 110–111. See page xvi for Teacher's Notes.

Picture Differences

A

- ◆ Sit with a partner and look at each other's papers.
- ◆ There are 10 differences between your pictures.
- ◆ Work with your partner to find the differences.

- ◆ Write the differences you find on the chart below.

A	B
1. computer on check-in counter	no computer on check-in counter
2.	
3.	
4.	
5.	
6.	
7.	
8.	
9.	
10.	

Fly Skyair

The Oxford Picture Dictionary, pages 105, 110–111. See page xvi for Teacher's Notes.

Picture Differences

B

- ◆ Sit with a partner and look at each other's papers.
- ◆ There are 10 differences between your pictures.
- ◆ Work with your partner to find the differences.

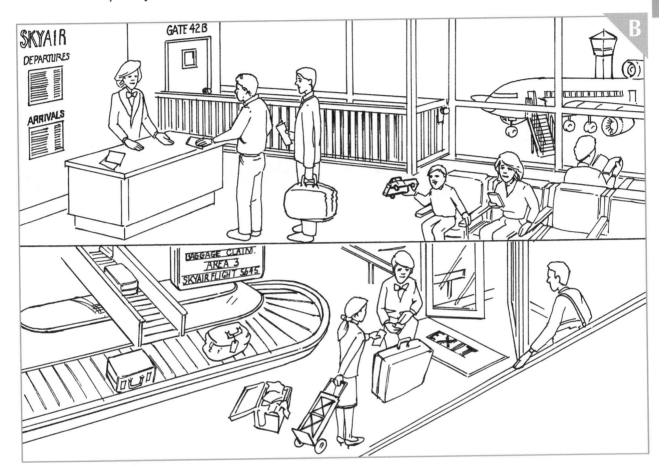

◆ Write the differences you find on the chart below.

A	B
1. computer on check-in counter	no computer on check-in counter
2.	
3.	
4.	
5.	
6.	
7.	
8.	
9.	
10.	

Destination San Francisco!

The Oxford Picture Dictionary, pages 104, 106. See page xviii for Teacher's Notes.

Information Exchange

A

1

- ◆ **Sit with a partner. (Don't show this paper to your partner!)**
- ◆ **Ask your partner about the missing information in the travel schedule below.**
- ◆ **You can use these questions:**

"What's the travel time on _____ ?"

"When does _____ leave?"

"When does _____ arrive?"

"How much is the fare on _____ ?"

- ◆ **Write in the missing information and read it back to your partner to check your work.**

GLOBAL TRAVEL — DESTINATION SAN FRANCISCO!

Prepared for: S. Lanzano
TRAVEL OPTIONS, departing 8/15:

Air/Ground	Leave	Arrive	Travel Time	Fare
Skyair Nonstop Flight 244	New York City <u>8:30</u> AM	San Francisco _____	5 Hrs.	round trip _____
Skyair Direct Flight 1069	New York City _____	Chicago 1:00 PM	_____	one way _____
Skyair Direct Flight 53	Chicago 1:05 PM	San Francisco	_____	one way $265.00
Intertrak Railways Line	New York City _____	San Francisco	75 Hrs. (arrive 8/18)	round trip _____

2

- ◆ **Use the sightseeing schedule below to answer your partner's questions.**

GLOBAL TRAVEL — SEE SAN FRANCISCO!

Prepared for: S. Lanzano

SIGHTSEEING OPTIONS: TRANSPORTATION	LEAVE	PLACE	TIME	COST
Bay City Lines – Bus Tours				
Basic Tour Downtown	10 AM, 12 PM, 2 PM, 4 PM	Lincoln Park NW Corner	2 Hrs.	$29.00
Deluxe Tour Bay Area	9:30 AM, 2:30 PM	Union Square SE Corner	3 Hrs.	$45.00
Golden Gate Travel – Ride the Trolley!				
Train Tours	Every 30 Min.	Mason/Powell Line	45 Min.	$12.00
Downtown San Francisco	9 AM – 5 PM	Broadway/Van Ness Line		
Embarcadero Lines – See Alcatraz and San Francisco from the Bay!				
Ferry Tours – Red Line	8 AM, 11 AM, 2 AM	Pier 17	1 Hr.	$25.00
Blue Line	9 AM, 12 PM, 3 PM	Pier 15	1 1/2 Hrs.	$34.00

- ◆ **What's next?** Pretend you are the traveler. Which transportation do you choose for going to San Francisco and for seeing the city? Think about money, time and how you like to travel. Discuss your choices with your partner.

Destination San Francisco!

The Oxford Picture Dictionary, pages 104, 106. See page xviii for Teacher's Notes.

1

◆ **Sit with a partner. (Don't show this paper to your partner!)**

◆ **Use the travel schedule below to answer your partner's questions.**

GLOBAL TRAVEL — DESTINATION SAN FRANCISCO!

Prepared for: S. Lanzano
TRAVEL OPTIONS, departing 8/15:

Air/Ground	Leave	Arrive	Travel Time	Fare
Skyair Nonstop Flight 244	New York City 8:30 AM	San Francisco 10:30 AM	5 Hrs.	round trip $525.00
Skyair Direct Flight 1069	New York City 11:30 AM	Chicago 1:00 PM	2 1/2 Hrs.	one way $129.00
Skyair Direct Flight 53	Chicago 1:05 PM	San Francisco 2:05 PM	3 Hrs.	one way $265.00
Intertrak Railways Line	New York City 9:00 PM	San Francisco 12:00 AM	75 Hrs. (arrive 8/18)	round trip $398.00

2

◆ **Ask your partner about the missing information on the sightseeing schedule below.**

◆ **You can use these questions:**

"When does the _____ tour start?"

"Where does the _____ tour leave from?"

"How long is the _____ tour?"

"How much is the tour?"

◆ **Write in the missing information and read it back to your partner to check your work.**

GLOBAL TRAVEL — SEE SAN FRANCISCO!

Prepared for: S. Lanzano

SIGHTSEEING OPTIONS: TRANSPORTATION	LEAVE	PLACE	TIME	COST
Bay City Lines – Bus Tours Basic Tour Downtown Deluxe Tour Bay Area	10 AM, 12 PM, 2 PM, 4 PM 9:30 AM, _____	Lincoln Park NW Corner Union Square SE Corner	2 Hrs. _____	_____ _____
Golden Gate Travel – Ride the Trolley! Train Tours Downtown San Francisco	Every_____ 9 AM – 5 PM	Mason/Powell Line_____ Broadway/Van Ness Line_____	45 Min.	_____
Embarcadero Lines – See Alcatraz and San Francisco from the Bay! Ferry Tours – Red Line Blue Line	8 AM, _____, 2 AM _____, 12 PM, 3 PM	Pier 17 Pier _____	1 Hr. 1 1/2 Hrs.	_____ $34.00

◆ **What's next?** Pretend you are the traveler. Which transportation do you choose for going to San Francisco and for seeing the city? Think about money, time and how you like to travel. Discuss your choices with your partner.

The Friendly Skies

The Oxford Picture Dictionary, pages 110–111. See page xix for Teacher's Notes.

Role Play

- ◆ Form groups of 4 people.
- ◆ Practice saying all the lines.
- ◆ Choose your character and decide what you will say.
- ◆ Think of other things your character can say.
- ◆ Act out your role play.

THE SCENE:
an airplane in flight

THE CHARACTERS:
a pilot
a flight attendant
a tired "frequent flyer"
a nervous passenger

THE PROPS:
a small carry-on bag
a blanket
a small tray
a glass
a napkin

THE SCRIPT:

Who says...	...these lines?
a flight attendant	Please put your bag in the overhead compartment.*
	What does this thing on the seat do?
	That opens up my tray table. Don't touch it!
	Hey, do you think this airplane is really safe?
	Sure. It's safer up here than in a car. Just relax.
	Excuse me. Could I change my seat? It's impossible to rest next to him!
	I'm sorry, but the flight is full. Would you like another drink?
	Captain, the passenger in 9A is very upset.
	Have him come to the cockpit in five minutes.
	Please fasten your seat belts and prepare to land.
	Land? I left my passport at the airport.
	Thanks for choosing Skyair on your flight to Chicago.

* You can substitute other vocabulary for the underlined words.

- ◆ **What's next?** Have the class arrange their seats into airplane rows and ask volunteer pilots and flight attendants to prepare "passengers" for take off. Have students talk to each other in-flight about where they are going and what they are going to do.

Drive a Car or Take Public Transportation?

The Oxford Picture Dictionary, pages 104, 106. See page xx for Teacher's Notes.

Take a Stand

- ♦ **Think about the reasons to drive a car or take public transportation.**
- ♦ **Read each statement on the list.**
- ♦ **If the statement shows that <u>driving a car</u> is a good idea, make a ✓ in that column.**
- ♦ **If the statement shows that <u>taking public transportation</u> is a good idea, make a ✓ in that column.**
- ♦ **For K and L, think of two more statements to add to this list.**

STATEMENTS	🚗	🚆
A. You can travel any time or place you want to go.		
B. Some companies give a bonus if you carpool with other workers.		
C. Auto insurance, registration, and gasoline can be expensive.		
D. Trains and subways almost always run on schedule.		
E. After work, it's easy to drive to the market, bank or school.		
F. Most traffic accidents are caused by passenger cars.		
G. Senior citizens and commuters save with special bus fares.		
H. Mass transit saves energy and can help reduce air pollution.		
I. You can read a book, have a snack, or sleep on a train or bus.		
J. Station wagons and minivans are great for families.		
K.		
L.		

- ♦ **Sit with a partner and compare papers.**
- ♦ **Write your and your partner's ideas.**

I think _____ *is better because* _____

_____.

My partner thinks _____ *is better because* _____

_____.

- ♦ **What's next?** Take a stand. Your teacher will tell you where to stand if you support driving a car and where to stand if you support taking public transportation.

Transportation Board.

tape here →

Draw
something you see on the highway. Describe it.

Name
something in a car that makes noise.

Pick a transportation card. Say 3 things about it.

Answer:
What kind of car or truck would you like to drive?

In 15 seconds...
tell how you get from school to home.

Act out
a transportation job for your group. (The group has to guess what it is!)

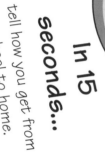

To begin...

- Put your markers on start.
- Take turns flipping a coin to move your marker around the board.

moves one space

moves two spaces

- Follow the directions on the squares.
- Ask your group for help when you don't know the answer.

Finish

Start

Pick a transportation picture card.

Spell it.

Name
something that makes a car safer to drive.

tape here →

Game

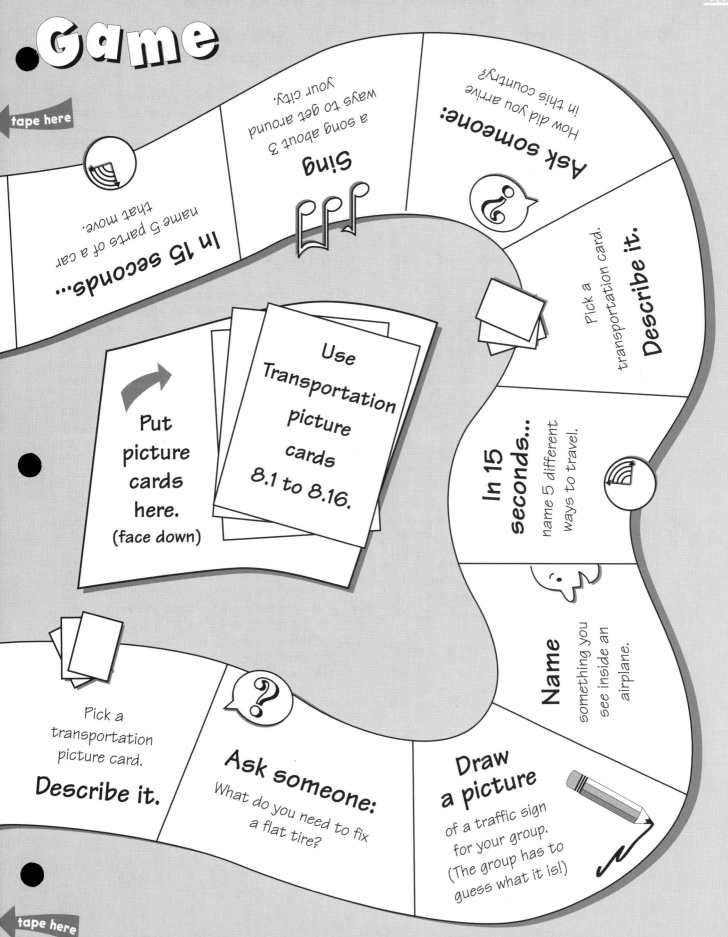

tape here

In 15 seconds...
name 5 parts of a car
that move.

Sing
a song about 3
ways to get around
your city.

Ask someone:
How did you arrive
in this country?

Pick a
transportation card.
Describe it.

Put
picture
cards
here.
(face down)

Use
Transportation
picture
cards
8.1 to 8.16.

In 15
seconds...
name 5 different
ways to travel.

Name
something you
see inside an
airplane.

Pick a
transportation
picture card.
Describe it.

Ask someone:
What do you need to fix
a flat tire?

**Draw
a picture**
of a traffic sign
for your group.
(The group has to
guess what it is!)

tape here

Transportation Picture Card Activities

MIXER (Whole Class)

Transportation People and Vehicles, page 129

1. Duplicate enough copies of the picture card page so that each student can have one card.

2. Give half of the students picture cards 8.1-8.8. These students need information about occupations. Give the other half picture cards 8.9-8.16. These are forms of transportation. Have all the transportation vehicles go to one side of the room and all the drivers/operators go to the other.

3. Have the students with transportation vehicles find the matching driver or operator by asking this question:

    When is this [bus] leaving?

    Students holding transportation occupations can answer:

    – *In five minutes.* or *At 11:00.*

    – *Sorry, I don't know. I'm not the bus driver.*

4. The activity ends when everyone finds a correct match.

PICK A PAIR (Pairs)

Car Parts and Maintenance, page 130

1. Pair students and give each pair one picture card page.

2. Have the pair cut up the cards, shuffle them and place them face down in four rows of four cards.

3. Have partners take turns turning over two cards at a time, trying to match related car parts and maintenance items. When one of each card is turned over, for example, *air and tires,* the student keeps the cards if she can make a sentence: *Air goes in the tires.* If the student can't say the sentence or the cards don't match (for example, *air/gas tank),* the student turns the cards back over.

4. The activity ends when all the cards are gone.

TWIN GRIDS (Pairs)

Directions and Traffic Signs Picture Cards, page 131
Grid, page 197

1. Duplicate one copy of the grid on page 197 and letter each square A-P. Give each student one grid and one picture card page. (If you have an overhead projector, see Using the Overhead Projector in the Picture Cards Teacher's Notes, page x.)

2. Have students cut apart their picture cards and place them face up, on their desks next to the grid.

3. Tell students to *put the stop sign on Avenue A.* Encourage students to ask clarification questions. *Did you say stop sign? Put it on Avenue A or E?,* etc.

4. Continue telling students where to put what until all the grid squares are filled. Have students compare their grids with one another as you clarify any discrepancies.

5. Next pair students. Give each pair a manila folder to use as a screen between the partners. Have one partner (the sender) tell the other (the receiver) where to put the different traffic signs. *Put the bus stop on Avenue C.* (Students do not have to use the same sentences you used.) Both partners place their pictures on the grids. When the grids are complete, senders and receivers compare their grids.

6. Have the senders and the receivers switch roles.

GUESS WHAT? (Groups)

Transportation Items Picture Cards, page 132

1. Have students form small groups of 3-4 students.

2. Give each group one page of cut-up picture cards. Have one student in the group shuffle the cards and place them face down on the table.

3. Each student takes a turn picking up the top picture card on the pile and giving a definition. *The price of a bus or plane trip.* (fare) Caution students to not use any part of the word in their definition. For example, they can't say, *Airplanes have these on their seats.* (seat belt)

4. The other group members try to guess the word. The first student to guess the word keeps the picture card.

5. The activity ends when all the cards are guessed correctly.

Picture Cards: Transportation People and Vehicles

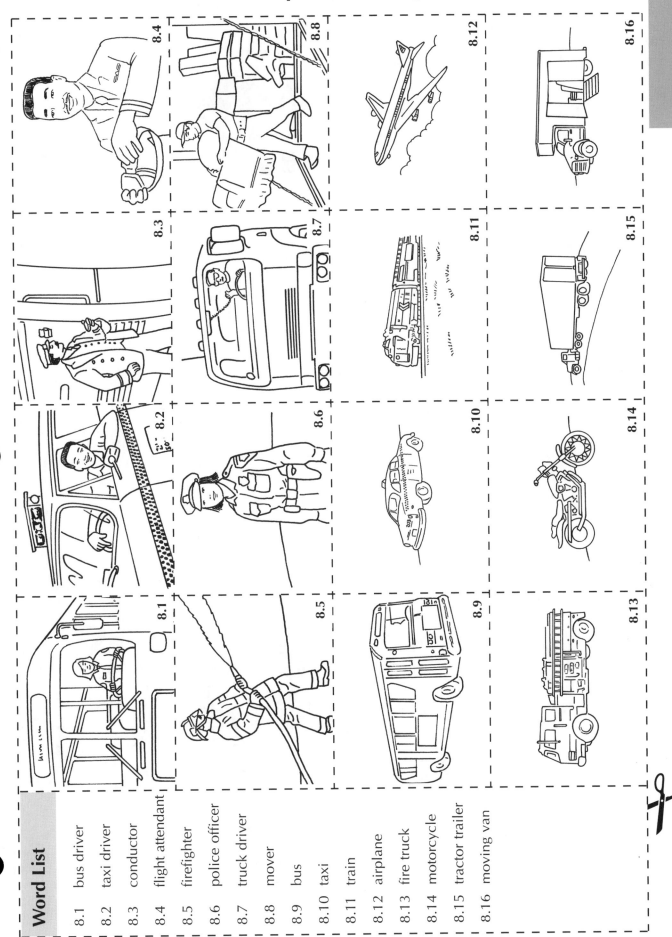

Word List

8.1	bus driver
8.2	taxi driver
8.3	conductor
8.4	flight attendant
8.5	firefighter
8.6	police officer
8.7	truck driver
8.8	mover
8.9	bus
8.10	taxi
8.11	train
8.12	airplane
8.13	fire truck
8.14	motorcycle
8.15	tractor trailer
8.16	moving van

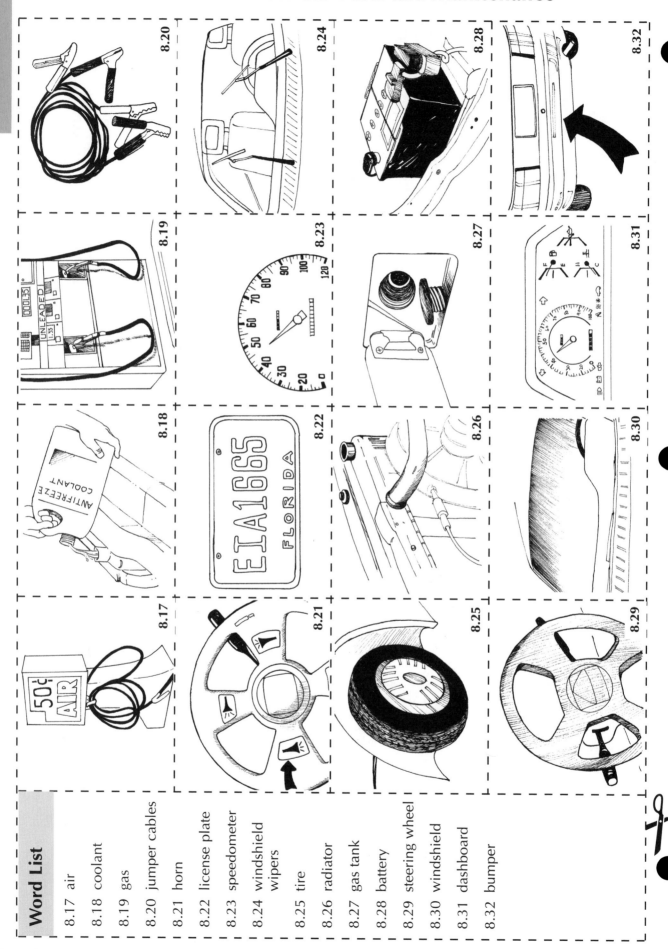

8.20

8.24

8.28

8.32

8.19

8.23

8.27

8.31

8.18

8.22

8.26

8.30

8.17

8.21

8.25

8.29

Word List

8.17 air

8.18 coolant

8.19 gas

8.20 jumper cables

8.21 horn

8.22 license plate

8.23 speedometer

8.24 windshield wipers

8.25 tire

8.26 radiator

8.27 gas tank

8.28 battery

8.29 steering wheel

8.30 windshield

8.31 dashboard

8.32 bumper

Picture Cards: Directions and Traffic Signs

ONE WAY — 8.36	pedestrian crossing — 8.40	handicapped — 8.44	airport — 8.48
SPEED LIMIT 35 — 8.35	ONLY — 8.39	SCHOOL XING — 8.43	car — 8.47
DO NOT ENTER / WRONG WAY — 8.34	NO OUTLET / DEAD END — 8.38	NO PARKING ANYTIME — 8.42	LOCAL 15 — 8.46
STOP — 8.33	U TURN OK — 8.37	RR crossing — 8.41	ONLY — 8.45

Word List

8.33 stop
8.34 wrong way
8.35 speed limit
8.36 one way
8.37 U-turn OK
8.38 dead end
8.39 right turn only
8.40 pedestrian crossing
8.41 railroad crossing
8.42 no parking
8.43 school crossing
8.44 handicapped parking
8.45 left turn only
8.46 bus stop
8.47 taxi stand
8.48 airport

Picture Cards: Transportation Items

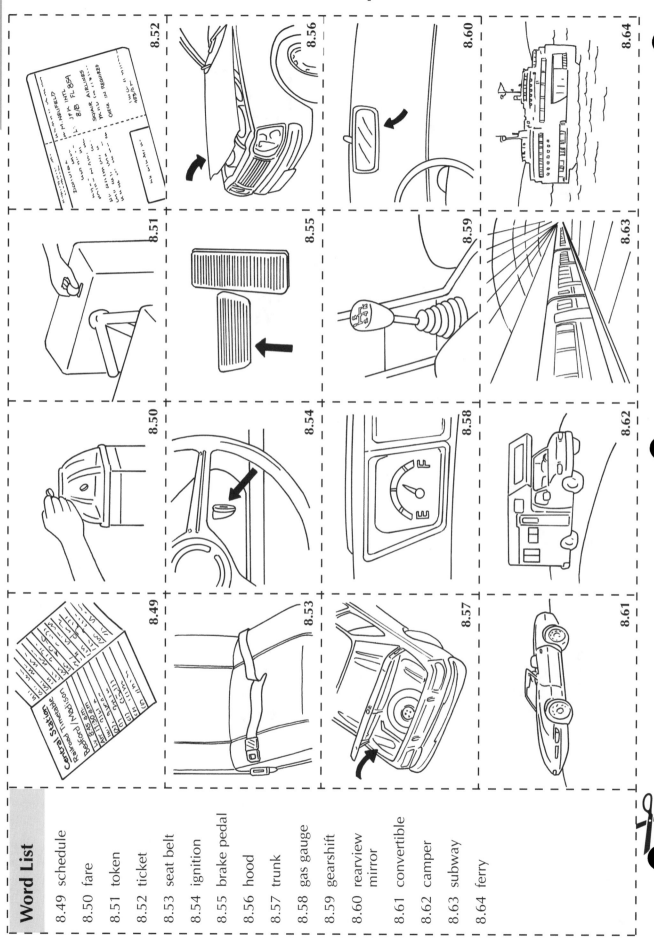

© 1999 Oxford University Press   Permission granted to reproduce for classroom use.

Word List

8.49 schedule
8.50 fare
8.51 token
8.52 ticket
8.53 seat belt
8.54 ignition
8.55 brake pedal
8.56 hood
8.57 trunk
8.58 gas gauge
8.59 gearshift
8.60 rearview mirror
8.61 convertible
8.62 camper
8.63 subway
8.64 ferry

Page(s)	Types of Schools (112)	English Composition (113)	U.S. History (114–115)	U.S. Government and Citizenship (116)	Geography (117)	Mathematics (118)	Science (119)	Music (120)	More School Subjects (121)	North America and Central America (122–123)	The World (124–125)	Energy and the Environment (126)	The Universe (127)
134 **Welcome to California!** (Round Table Label)					♦								
135 **What do you like to do?** (Mixer)		♦	♦			♦	♦	♦					
136–137 **He did what??!!** (Information Exchange)			♦							♦	♦		
138–139 **Government and Citizenship Puzzle** (Double Crossword)			♦										
140 **Time for Class** (Role Play)		♦											
141 **Space Exploration— Yes or No?** (Take a Stand)							♦					♦	♦
142–143 **Areas of Study Board Game** (Board Game)	♦	♦	♦	♦	♦	♦	♦	♦	♦	♦	♦	♦	♦
144–148 **Picture Card Activities and Picture Cards**					♦	♦		♦	♦				♦

Welcome to California!

The Oxford Picture Dictionary, page 117. See page xii for Teacher's Notes.

◆ **Form groups of 4 people.**

◆ **Each person in the group takes turns labeling the places in the travel poster.**

◆ **After all the places have labels, look in the *Dictionary* to check your group's work.**

◆ **What's next?** What places in your country are popular for vacations? Draw a travel poster showing a geographical area that tourists would like to see. Describe it to your group.

What do you like to do?

The Oxford Picture Dictionary, pages 113–115, 118–121. See page xiii for Teacher's Notes.

Mixer

- ◆ **Write the missing letters for each word.**
- ◆ **Walk around the room. Ask and answer the questions.**
- ◆ **Write a different name in each box.**

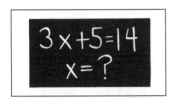

1. Do you like solving <u>m</u> <u>a</u> <u>t</u> <u>h</u> problems?

Yes	No

2. Do you like listening to an <u>o</u> _ _ _ _ _ _ _ _ ?

Yes	No

3. Do you like working with <u>c</u> _ _ _ _ _ _ _ ?

Yes	No

4. Do you like doing <u>s</u> _ _ _ _ _ _ _ experiments?

Yes	No

5. Do you like doing <u>a</u> _ _ _ projects?

Yes	No

6. Do you like writing <u>c</u> _ _ _ _ _ _ _ _ _ _ _ ?

Yes	No

7. Do you like reading about <u>h</u> _ _ _ _ _ _ ?

Yes	No

- ◆ **What's next?** What's your favorite school subject? Pretend you are an expert and teach a one-minute lesson to your classmates.

He did what??!!

The Oxford Picture Dictionary, pages 114–115, 122–125. See page xviii for Teacher's Notes. | **Information Exchange**

A

1

◆ **Sit with a partner. (Don't show this paper to your partner!)**

◆ **Ask your partner about the missing information on the chart below.**

◆ **You can use these questions:**

"What did _____ explore?"

"Where was _____ from?"

"When did _____ explore it?""

◆ **Write in the missing information and read it back to your partner to check your work.**

AMAZING DISCOVERIES

EXPLORER	AREA EXPLORED	DATE	COUNTRY
Christopher Columbus	_____	1492	Italy
Ponce de Leon	_____	1513	_____
Henry Hudson	Canada	_____	_____
Samuel de Champlain	_____	_____	France
Vitus Bering	_____	1741	_____
Francisco Coronado	Southwest U.S.	–	_____
Robert Peary	_____	1892	U.S.A.

2

◆ **Use the chart below to answer your partner's questions.**

INCREDIBLE INVENTIONS

INVENTOR	INVENTION	DATE	COUNTRY
Thomas Edison	phonograph	1877	U.S.A.
Guglielmo Marconi	radio	1895	Italy
Alexander Graham Bell	telephone	1876	U.S.A.
John K. Baird	television	1926	England
Hitachi Company	CD ROM	1985	Japan
Karl Benz	automobile	1885	Germany
Howard Aiken	computer	1944	U.S.A.

◆ **What's next?** Work with your partner to draw an invention that will make learning English easier.

He did what??!!

The Oxford Picture Dictionary, pages 114–115, 122–125. See page xviii for Teacher's Notes. Information Exchange

B

- ◆ **Sit with a partner. (Don't show this paper to your partner!)**
- ◆ **Use the chart to answer your partner's questions.**

AMAZING DISCOVERIES

EXPLORER	AREA EXPLORED	DATE	COUNTRY
Christopher Columbus	West Indies	1492	Italy
Ponce de Leon	Florida	1513	Spain
Henry Hudson	Canada	1610	England
Samuel de Champlain	Maine	1604	France
Vitus Bering	Alaska	1741	Denmark
Francisco Coronado	Southwest U.S.	1540 – 1542	Spain
Robert Peary	Greenland	1892	U.S.A.

- ◆ **Ask your partner about the missing information on the chart below.**
- ◆ **You can use these questions:**

  "What did _____ invent?"

  "Where did _____ invent it?"

  "When did _____ invent it?"

- ◆ **Write in the missing information and read it back to your partner to check your work.**

INCREDIBLE INVENTIONS

INVENTOR	INVENTION	DATE	COUNTRY
Thomas Edison	phonograph		
Guglielmo Marconi			Italy
Alexander Graham Bell		1876	
John K. Baird	television		
Hitachi Company		1985	
Karl Benz	automobile		
Howard Aiken			U.S.A.

- ◆ **What's next?** Work with your partner to draw an invention that will make learning English easier.

Government and Citizenship Puzzle

The Oxford Picture Dictionary, pages 114–115. See page xvii for Teacher's Notes. **Double Crossword**

A

- ◆ **Sit with a partner. (Don't show this paper to your partner!)**
- ◆ **Take turns giving the clues to complete the puzzle.**

  1 down —The people who serve on the Supreme Court

- ◆ **If your partner needs help, give one letter from the answer on your puzzle.**

  The second letter is U.

- ◆ **When both puzzles are complete, compare your work.**

Clues

1 down — The people who serve on the Supreme Court

2 down — The branch of the government with the senate

4 down — This is where senators work

6 down — This is what you do to the law

7 down — The number of years you must be in the U.S. to become a citizen

9 down — This is every citizen's responsibility and right

10 down — The color of the President's house

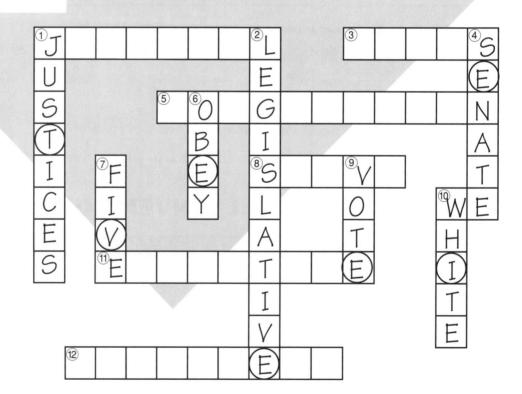

- ◆ **What's next?** Work with your partner to unscramble the letters in the circles to find the word that means a congressman or congresswoman.

Government and Citizenship Puzzle

The Oxford Picture Dictionary, pages 114–115. See page xvii for Teacher's Notes.

Double Crossword

B

- ◆ **Sit with a partner. (Don't show this paper to your partner!)**
- ◆ **Take turns giving the clues to complete the puzzle.**

  1 across — The branch of the government that includes the Supreme Court

- ◆ **If your partner needs help, give one letter from the answer on your puzzle.**

  The second letter is U.

- ◆ **When both puzzles are complete, compare your work.**

Clues

1 across — The branch of the government that includes the Supreme Court

3 across — What you pay the government

5 across — This is a senator or a representative

8 across — Another way to say "be" on a jury

10 across — The first word in the Constitution

11 across — The branch of the government that includes the President

12 across — The head of the United States government

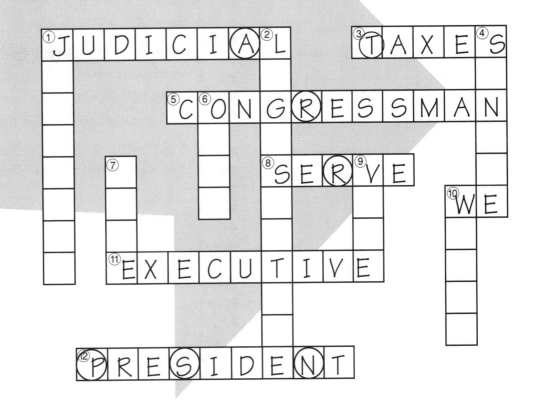

- ◆ **What's next?** Work with your partner to unscramble the letters in the circles to find the word that means a congressman or congresswoman.

Time for Class

Role Play

- ◆ **Form groups of 4 people.**
- ◆ **Practice saying all the lines.**
- ◆ **Choose your character and decide what you will say.**
- ◆ **Think of other things your character can say.**
- ◆ **Act out your role play.**

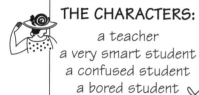

THE CHARACTERS:
a teacher
a very smart student
a confused student
a bored student

THE SCENE:
A classroom where an English teacher tries to explain punctuation to her class. Three students ask questions and make comments.

THE PROPS:
some chalk
a blackboard
three chairs

THE SCRIPT:

Who says...	...these lines?
a teacher	Today we're going to talk about punctuation*.
	What time is this class over?
	I know that a period comes at the end of a sentence.
	Could you explain again about colons?
	Do you have any gum?
	Come up to the board and underline the punctuation.
	Who would like to correct the question?
	There's a mistake on the board. There should be a question mark.
	I'm so confused!
	Take out your pencils and paper. I'm going to dictate a sentence.

* You can substitute other vocabulary for the underlined words.

- ◆ **What's next?** Write sentences with your group using all the punctuation from page 113 in the *Dictionary*. Write one of your group's sentences on the board and explain the punctuation.

Space Exploration—Yes or No?

The Oxford Picture Dictionary, pages 119, 126–127. See page xx for Teacher's Notes.

Take a Stand

- ◆ **Think about the reasons to explore space.**
- ◆ **Read each statement on the list.**
- ◆ **If the statement shows that space exploration is <u>a good idea</u>, make a ✔ in that column.**
- ◆ **If the statement shows that space exploration is <u>not a good idea</u>, make a ✔ in that column.**
- ◆ **For K and L, think of two more statements to add to this list.**

STATEMENTS	+	–
A. Space stations can do experiments about conditions on other planets.		
B. Many countries don't have enough money for health and job programs.		
C. The world's temperature and climate are changing because of pollution.		
D. Most planets are not able to support life.		
E. Some countries have too many people living in them.		
F. Countries with space programs are respected by other countries.		
G. Space programs cost a lot of money.		
H. Many people dream of visiting another planet or want to live there.		
I. Satellites can record results showing changes in the earth.		
J. Nobody knows for sure if there is life on other planets.		
K.		
L.		

- ◆ **Sit with a partner and compare papers.**
- ◆ **Write your and your partner's ideas.**

I think space exploration is a _____ *idea because* _____

_____.

My partner thinks space exploration is a _____ *idea because* _____

_____.

- ◆ **What's next?** Take a stand. Your teacher will tell you where to stand if you support space exploration and where to stand if you don't support space exploration.

Areas of Study Board.

tape here

Draw
a continent and label 3 places on it.

In 15 seconds...
name 3 things in a science laboratory.

Pick a shapes picture card. Say 3 things about it.

Answer:
What can you do to save energy?

In 15 seconds...
name 3 punctuation marks.

Act out
playing a musical instrument. (The group has to guess what it is!)

To begin...
- Put your markers on start.
- Take turns flipping a coin to move your marker around the board.

moves one space

moves two spaces

- Follow the directions on the squares.
- Ask your group for help when you don't know the answer.

Finish

Start

Pick a shapes picture card.
Spell it.

Name
something you see in the sky.

tape here

Game

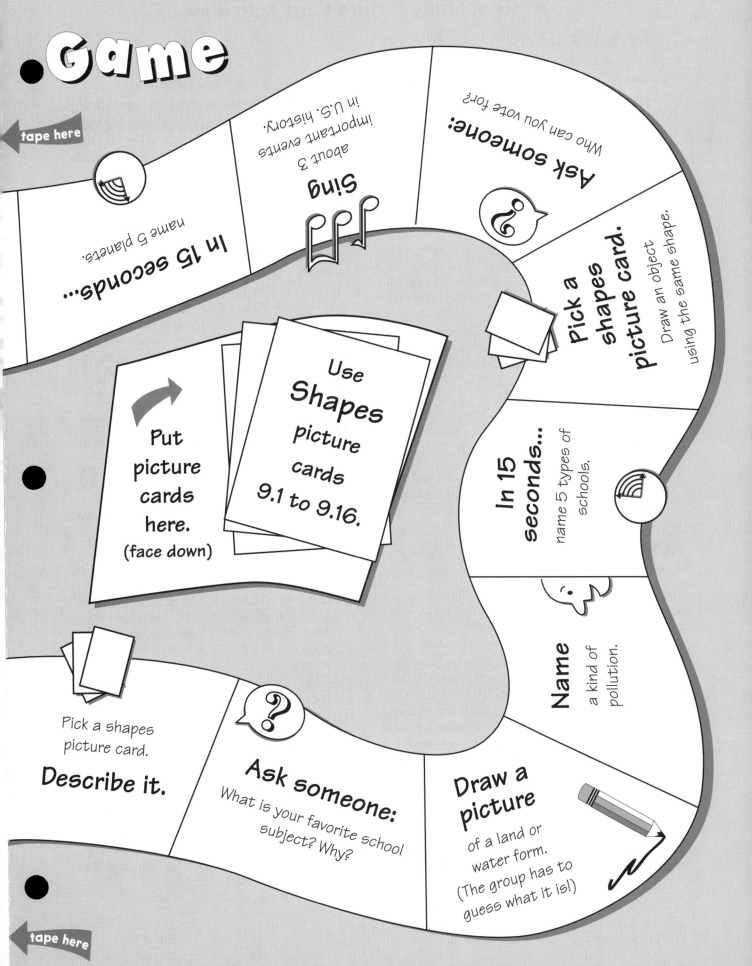

tape here

In 15 seconds...
name 5 planets.

Sing
about 3 important events in U.S. history.

Ask someone:
Who can you vote for?

Pick a shapes picture card.
Draw an object using the same shape.

Put picture cards here.
(face down)

Use Shapes picture cards 9.1 to 9.16.

In 15 seconds...
name 5 types of schools.

Name a kind of pollution.

Pick a shapes picture card.
Describe it.

Ask someone:
What is your favorite school subject? Why?

Draw a picture of a land or water form.
(The group has to guess what it is!)

tape here

Areas of Study Picture Card Activities

TWIN GRIDS (Pairs)

Shapes Picture Cards, page 145
Grid, page 197

1. Duplicate one copy of the blank grid on page 197. Write the letters A-D across the top of the paper, and the numbers 1-4 down the left side of the paper. Give each student one grid and one picture card page. (If you have an overhead projector, see Using the Overhead Projector in the Picture Cards Teacher's Notes, page x.)

2. Have students cut apart their picture card pages and place them face up, on their desks next to the grid.

3. Tell students to find the triangle. Direct students to place the picture of the triangle on the grid square marked B-2. Encourage students to ask clarification questions. *Did you say triangle or angle? Was that A-2 or B-2?*

4. Continue telling students where to put what until all the grid squares are filled. Have students compare their grids with one another as you clarify any discrepancies.

5. Next pair students. Give each pair a manila folder to use as a screen between the partners. Have one partner (the sender) tell the other (the receiver), *Put the square on C-4.* (Students do not have to copy your sentences.) Both partners place their pictures on the grids. When the grids are complete, senders and receivers compare their grids.

6. Have senders and receivers switch roles.

PICK A PAIR (Pairs)

Musical Instruments Picture Cards, page 146

1. Pair students and give each pair one picture card page.

2. Have the pair cut up the cards, shuffle them and place them face down in four rows of four cards.

3. Have partners take turns turning over two cards at a time, trying to match two musical instruments in the same "family" (strings, brass, etc.) When the cards match, for example, *violin/guitar*, the student keeps the cards if she can make a sentence comparing both pictures, *Violin and guitar both have strings.* When the student can't say the sentence or the cards don't match, (for example, *violin/flute*) the student turns the cards back over.

4. The activity ends when all the cards are gone.

PICK AND CHOOSE (Groups)

School Subjects Picture Cards, page 147

1. Have students form groups of 2-4 students.

2. Give each group one copy of the picture card page. Have them cut apart the pictures and place them in random rows, face up on the table.

3. Tell students that they will be choosing school subjects that will help people in different jobs.

3. Announce the first round of play. *The first job is: taxi driver. Your group has two minutes to pick and choose four school subjects that provide the best experience for a taxi driver.*

4. Walk around, encouraging students to discuss their choices and monitoring to make sure everyone has a chance to pick a school subject for the job.

5. Call time and survey the class to find out the most popular school subjects. Continue play using different job titles.

6. To vary the activity, distribute a page of the Occupations Picture Cards, page 177. Have students cut up the picture cards and try to match school subjects with jobs. Put one or two model sentences on the board for students to copy. *An actor needs a theater arts class. A carpenter needs a class in geometry.*

PEER DICTATION (Pairs)

Earth and Space Picture Cards, page 148

1. Duplicate a class set of the picture card pages and cut off the Word List on the sidebar. [Hold on to these for step 6.]

2. Pair students and give Student A and Student B each a picture card page. Have Student A put the page face down until it is his turn.

3. Direct Student B in each pair to look at page 117 in the *Dictionary* and read off the list of Geography words. When Student A hears a word that is on his picture card page they say *I have that. How do you spell it?* Student B spells out the word so that Student A can write it under the picture.

4. When Student A has written all the Geography words, he put his papers aside. B then gets a picture card page and listens to Student A read off the list of Universe words from page 127 in the *Dictionary*. He writes the names of the Universe words under those pictures.

5. Both students then write the words for the pictures not yet labeled (Student A writes down the Universe words, Student B writes down the Geography words.) They then compare their answers.

6. Distribute the class set of the cut Word List and have students check the correct spelling of all the pictures on their pages.

Picture Cards: Shapes

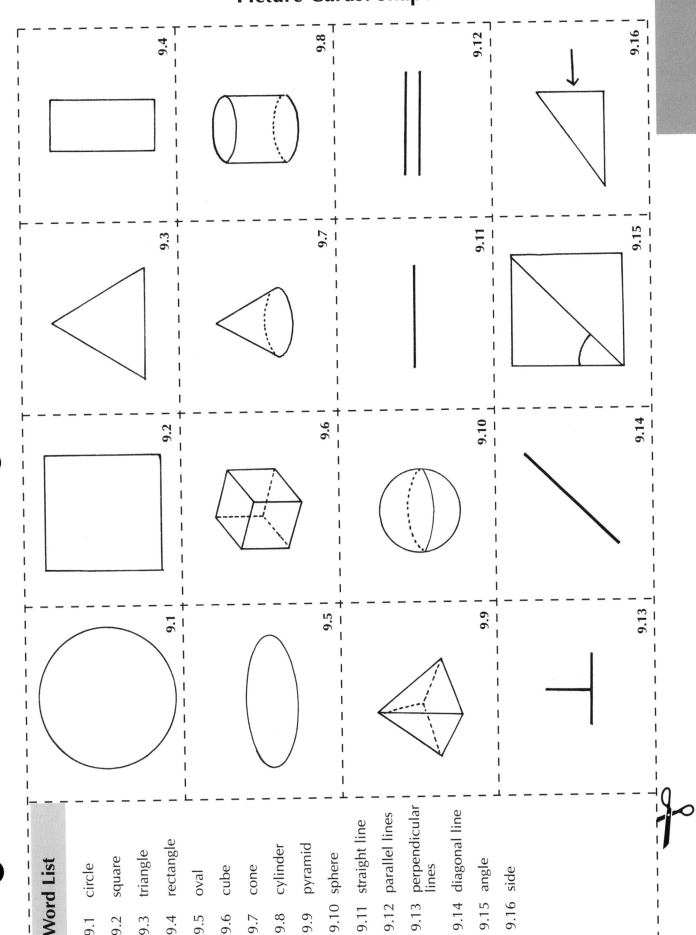

9.4	**9.8**	**9.12**	**9.16**
9.3	**9.7**	**9.11**	**9.15**
9.2	**9.6**	**9.10**	**9.14**
9.1	**9.5**	**9.9**	**9.13**

Word List

9.1   circle
9.2   square
9.3   triangle
9.4   rectangle
9.5   oval
9.6   cube
9.7   cone
9.8   cylinder
9.9   pyramid
9.10 sphere
9.11 straight line
9.12 parallel lines
9.13 perpendicular
       lines
9.14 diagonal line
9.15 angle
9.16 side

Picture Cards: Musical Instruments

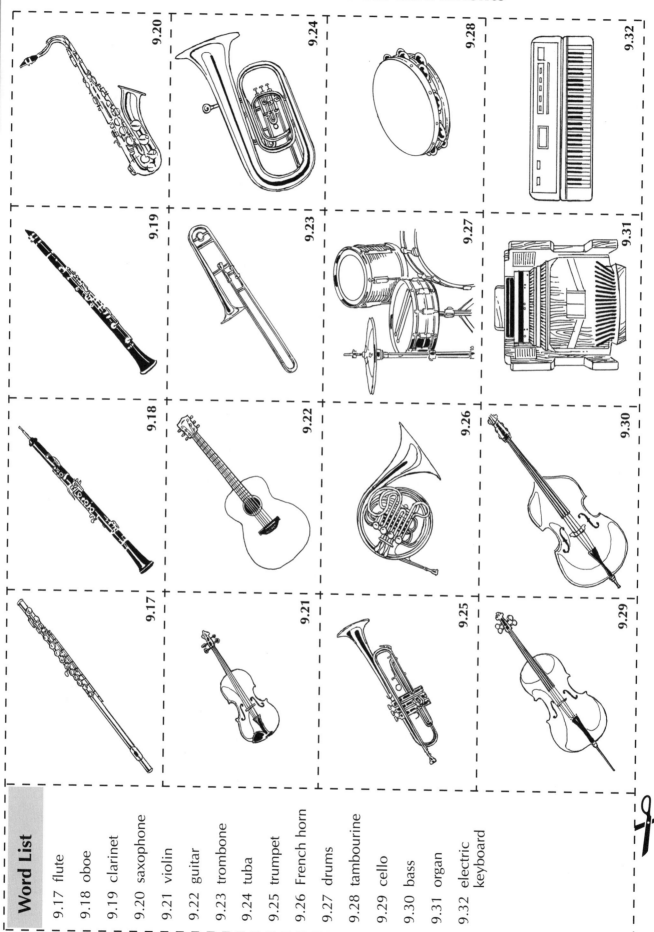

9.20
9.24
9.28
9.32
9.19
9.23
9.27
9.31
9.18
9.22
9.26
9.30
9.17
9.21
9.25
9.29

Word List

9.17 flute
9.18 oboe
9.19 clarinet
9.20 saxophone
9.21 violin
9.22 guitar
9.23 trombone
9.24 tuba
9.25 trumpet
9.26 French horn
9.27 drums
9.28 tambourine
9.29 cello
9.30 bass
9.31 organ
9.32 electric
     keyboard

Picture Cards: School Subjects

Picture Cards: Earth and Space

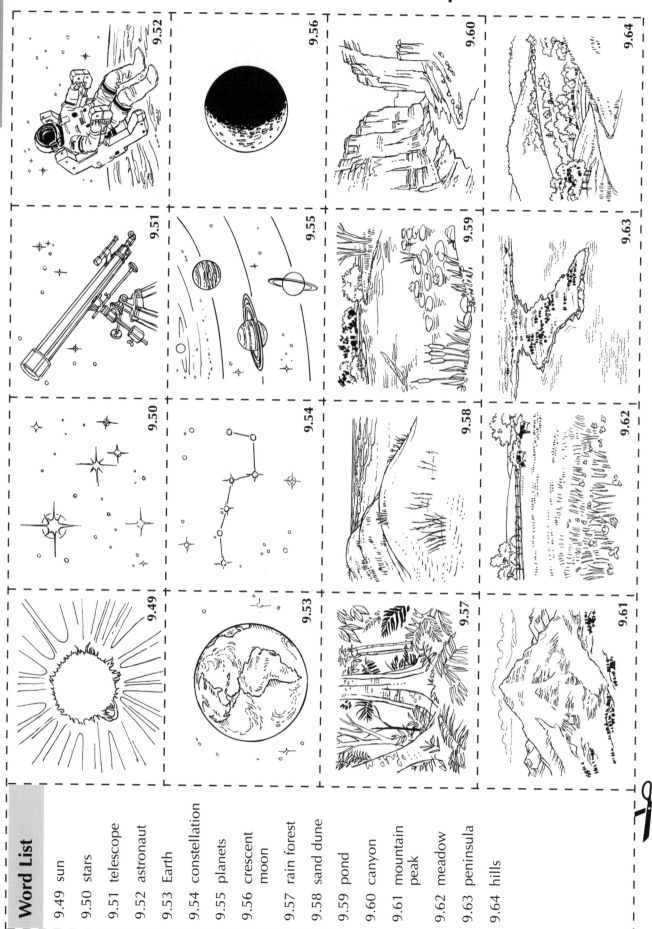

9.52

9.56

9.60

9.64

9.51

9.55

9.59

9.63

9.50

9.54

9.58

9.62

9.49

9.53

9.57

9.61

Word List

9.49 sun
9.50 stars
9.51 telescope
9.52 astronaut
9.53 Earth
9.54 constellation
9.55 planets
9.56 crescent moon
9.57 rain forest
9.58 sand dune
9.59 pond
9.60 canyon
9.61 mountain peak
9.62 meadow
9.63 peninsula
9.64 hills

Page(s)		Trees and Plants (128)	Flowers (129)	Marine Life, Amphibians, and Reptiles (130–131)	Birds, Insects, Arachnids (132)	Domestic Animals and Rodents (133)	Mammals (134–135)
150	**Greenthumbs Nursery** (Round Table Label)	◆	◆		◆		
151	**The pet store is open.** (Survey)			◆		◆	
152–153	**Under the Sea** (Picture Differences)			◆			
154–155	**Animal Kingdom** (Double Crossword)						◆
156	**Sunday at the Zoo** (Role Play)	◆	◆	◆	◆	◆	
157	**A Dog or a Cat?** (Take a Stand)						
158–159	**Plants and Animals Board Game** (Board Game)					◆	
160–164	**Picture Card Activities and Picture Cards**	◆	◆	◆	◆	◆	◆

Greenthumbs Nursery

The Oxford Picture Dictionary, pages 128–129, 132. See page xii for Teacher's Notes.

- ◆ **Form groups of 4 people.**
- ◆ **Each person in the group takes turns labeling the items on this paper.**
- ◆ **After all the pictures have labels, look in the *Dictionary* to check your group's work.**

seed

- ◆ **What's next?** Make a nature scrapbook with your group. Bring your notebook, pencil and a paper bag. Collect samples or draw pictures of trees, plants, birds and insects you find near your school. Assemble your scrapbook and share your discoveries with the class.

The pet store is open.

The Oxford Picture Dictionary, pages 130–131, 133. See page xiv for Teacher's Notes.

◆ **Read the survey questions and mark your answers with a ✔.**

◆ **Ask and answer the questions again with nine classmates.**

◆ **Mark your classmates' answers on the survey form.**

Do you prefer...

		My Answers	My Classmates' Answers	No Opinion
...a goldfish or a rabbit?	a. goldfish			
	b. rabbit			
...a kitten or a puppy?	a. kitten			
	b. puppy			
...a cat or a guinea pig?	a. cat			
	b. guinea pig			
...a lizard or a turtle?	a. lizard			
	b. turtle			
...a frog or a mouse?	a. frog			
	b. mouse			
...a snake or a parakeet?	a. snake			
	b. parakeet			

◆ **Complete the graph below. Chart only student preferences.**

a   b   (Note: Your chart will not show the "No opinion" category.)

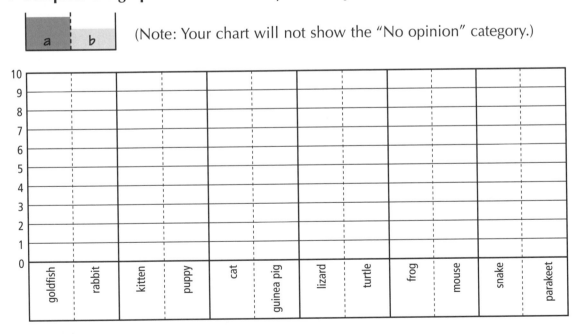

◆ **What's next?** Your teacher will ask you for your survey results. Write sentences about the answers. Follow the example below:

Seven out of ten students prefer a goldfish to a rabbit.

Under the Sea

A

- ◆ Sit with a partner and look at each other's papers.
- ◆ There are 10 differences between your pictures.
- ◆ Work with your partner to find the differences.

◆ **Write the differences you find on the chart.**

A	B
1. one swordfish	two swordfish
2.	
3.	
4.	
5.	
6.	
7.	
8.	
9.	
10.	

Under the Sea

The Oxford Picture Dictionary, pages 130–131. See page xvi for Teacher's Notes.

◆ **Sit with a partner and look at each other's papers.**

◆ **There are 10 differences between your pictures.**

◆ **Work with your partner to find the differences.**

◆ **Write the differences you find on the chart.**

A	B
1. one swordfish	two swordfish
2.	
3.	
4.	
5.	
6.	
7.	
8.	
9.	
10.	

Animal Kingdom

The Oxford Picture Dictionary, pages 134–135. See page xvii for Teacher's Notes.

Double Crossword

A

♦ **Sit with a partner. (Don't show this paper to your partner!)**
♦ **Take turns giving the clues to complete the puzzle.**

   1 down — I have a black mask like a crook. I wash my food, but never cook.

♦ **If your partner needs help, give one letter from the answer on your puzzle.**

   The first letter is R.

♦ **When both puzzles are complete, compare your work.**

Clues

1 down — I have a black mask like a crook. I wash my food, but never cook.

2 down — I always love to play around. I'm the smartest ape in town.

3 down — I'm like a hairy buffalo. On the western plains I go.

4 down — I'm black and white. My nose is pink. When I get mad, I really stink.

5 down — My neck's like a camel, my eyes like a doe. I live in the Andes, in Chile, you know.

6 down — My black spots make me look unique. I'm a cat who's fast and sleek.

10 down — All day, I'm hanging upside down. At night, I'm flying all around.

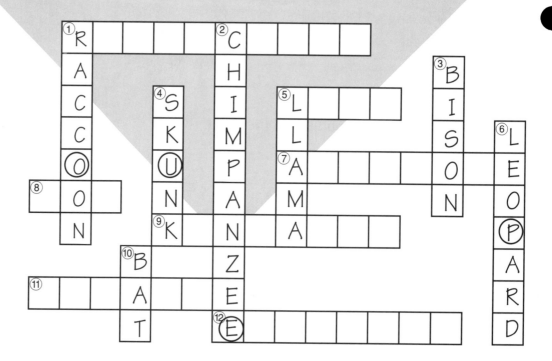

♦ **What's next?** Work with your partner to unscramble the letters in the circles to spell an animal's name. Clue: Please don't bump into me!

Animal Kingdom

B

◆ **Sit with a partner. (Don't show this paper to your partner!)**

◆ **Take turns giving the clues to complete the puzzle.**

   1 across — I have a horn that grows and grows. It sits on my tremendous nose.

◆ **If your partner needs help, give one letter from the answer on your puzzle.**

   The second letter is H.

◆ **When both puzzles are complete, compare your work.**

Clues

1 across — I have a horn that grows and grows. It sits on my tremendous nose.

5 across — King of the Jungle is my name. I roar and have a shaggy mane.

7 across — I have antlers by the dozen. Rudolph is my red-nosed cousin.

8 across — When I hunt, I'm sly and quick. I catch chickens with my tricks.

9 across — Across Australia, see me jump. I have a pouch, but not a hump.

11 across — I'm the tallest on four feet. I eat leaves. I don't eat meat.

12 across — My tusks are long. My trunk is too. I'm in the circus and the zoo.

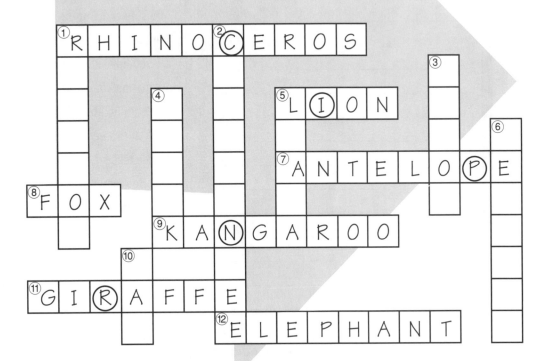

◆ **What's next?** Work with your partner to unscramble the letters in the circles to spell an animal's name. Clue: Please don't bump into me!

Sunday at the Zoo

Role Play

- ◆ Form groups of 4 people.
- ◆ Practice saying all the lines.
- ◆ Choose your character and decide what you will say.
- ◆ Think of other things your character can say.
- ◆ Act out your role play.

THE CHARACTERS:
a parent
a child
a tour guide
a gift shop clerk

THE SCENE:
a zoo

THE PROPS:
a soft drink can
a T-shirt
a small flowering plant

THE SCRIPT:

Who says...	...these lines?
a child	What are these trees? Their branches* are beautiful.
	Those are willow trees. They grow very well here.
	Can I pet the baby sheep?
	You sure can. But the petting zoo closes in five minutes.
	Do you have any books about dolphins?
	All marine life books are 25% off for zoo members.
	I'm learning about birds in school.
	Look at this eagle. It has unusual feathers.
	Please take your soda outside. No drinks are allowed.
	O.K. But can I buy this spider T-shirt first?
	Would you like a free daisy plant with your book?
	Ah-choo! No thanks, I'm allergic to daisies.

* You can substitute other vocabulary for the underlined words.

- ◆ **What's next?** Work with your group to plan a zoo for your city. Decide which plants, animals and special attractions you want to include. Draw a "map" showing your plan and present it to the class.

A Dog or a Cat?

The Oxford Picture Dictionary, page 133. See page xx for Teacher's Notes.   **Take a Stand**

- ◆ **Think about the reasons to own a dog or a cat.**
- ◆ **Read each statement on the list.**
- ◆ **If the statement shows that <u>owning a dog</u> is a good idea, make a check ✔ in that column.**
- ◆ **If the statement shows that <u>owning a cat</u> is a good idea, make a check ✔ in that column.**
- ◆ **For K and L, think of two more statements to add to this list.**

STATEMENTS	dog	cat
A. Cats can live indoors in small apartments.		
B. Many dogs bark when their owners are away from home.		
C. You can teach a dog to play games or tricks, like catching a frisbee.		
D. Cat food is inexpensive.		
E. Some cats like to scratch their claws on furniture and doors.		
F. A dog can protect your home and family.		
G. Cats are independent and don't need a lot of attention.		
H. You never have to walk a cat.		
I. Dogs make good companions for lonely people.		
J. Walking the dog is good exercise.		
K.		
L.		

- ◆ **Sit with a partner and compare papers.**
- ◆ **Write your and your partner's ideas.**

I think _____ *are good pets because* _____

_____ .

My partner thinks _____ *are good pets because* _____

_____ .

- ◆ **What's next?** Take a stand. Your teacher will tell you where to stand if you support owning a dog and where to stand if you support owning a cat.

Plants and Animals Board

Draw
something
you see in a
garden.
Describe it.

Name
a dangerous plant
or animal. How
can it hurt you?

Pick an
animal card.
Say 3 things
about it.

Answer:
What animal do
countries protect?
Why?

**In 15
seconds...**
name 5 animals that
live in water.

Act out
an animal for your
group. Don't make a
sound. (The group has
to guess what it is!)

To begin...
- Put your markers on start.
- Take turns flipping a coin to move your
  marker around the board.

moves
one
space

moves
two
spaces

- Follow the directions on the squares.
- Ask your group for help when you
  don't know the answer.

Finish

Start

Pick an animal card.
Spell it.

Name
an animal you see
every day.

Game

tape here

In 15 seconds...
name 3 different parts of a bird.

Sing
a song about animals on a farm.

Ask someone:
What's your favorite...?

Pick an animal card.
Describe it.

Put picture cards here.
(face down)

Use Animal picture cards 10.1 to 10.16.

In 15 seconds...
name 3 different parts of a tree.

Name
a marine animal that you eat.

Pick an animal card.
Describe it.

Ask someone:
What animal are you afraid of? Why?

Draw a picture
of an animal for your group. (The group has to guess what it is.)

tape here

Plants and Animals Picture Card Activities

PICK AND CHOOSE (Groups)

Pets and Farm Animals Picture Cards, page 161

1. Have students form groups of 2-4 students.

2. Give each group one copy of the picture card pages and a piece of blank paper. Have them cut apart the pictures and place them in random rows, face up on the table.

3. Tell students that they will be choosing different animals for various situations.

3. Announce the first round of play. *You have a farm. Your group has two minutes to pick and choose four animals that are best for your farm.*

4. Walk around, encouraging students to discuss their choices and monitoring to make sure everyone has a chance to pick an animal that they feel is the best.

5. Call time and survey the class to find out the most popular animals. Continue play using different situations such as: 1) best animals for an apartment 2) best animals for a 5-year-old child 3) "smartest" animals, 4) "noisiest" animals, etc.

6. To vary the activity, have students take turns picking a picture card from a pile and acting it out for the group. The charade can include a description of the animal or animal sound.

PICK A PAIR I (Pairs)

Plants and Animals Picture Cards, page 162

1. Pair students and give each pair one picture card page.

2. Have the pair cut up the cards, shuffle them and place them face down in four rows of four cards.

3. Have partners take turns turning over two cards at a time, trying to match related plants and animals (trees, plants, reptiles, mammals, birds, etc.) When the cards match, for example, *whale/seal,* the student keeps the cards if she can make a sentence: *Whales and seals are sea mammals.* When the student can't say the sentence or the cards don't match, the student turns the cards back over.

4. The activity ends when all the cards are gone.

TWIN GRIDS (Pairs)

Mammals Picture Cards, page 163
Grid, page 197

1. Duplicate one copy of the grid on page 197. Write in 16 numbers, one number per square. Give each student one grid and one picture card page. (If you have an overhead projector, see Using the Overhead Projector in the Picture Cards Teachers' Notes, page x.)

2. Have students cut apart their picture cards and place them face up on their desks next to the grid.

3. Tell students that each numbered box represents an area for animals in a zoo. Direct students to find the picture of the lion, and place this picture on the grid square with #1 in it. Encourage students to ask clarification questions. *Did you say lion or llama? Was that #1 or #11?*

4. Continue telling students where to put what until all the grid squares are filled. Have students compare their grids with one another as you clarify any discrepancies.

5. Next pair students. Give each pair a manila folder to use as a screen between the partners. Have one partner (the sender) tell the other (the receiver), *Put the lion in area #1.* [Students do not have to copy your sentences.] Both partners place their pictures on the grids. When the grids are complete, senders and receivers compare their grids.

6. Have senders and receivers switch roles.

PICK A PAIR II (Pairs)

Animals/Animal Parts Picture Cards, page 164

1. Pair students and give each pair one picture card page.

2. Have the pair cut up the cards, shuffle them and place them face down in four rows of four cards.

3. Have partners take turns turning over two cards at a time, trying to match various animals with their corresponding animal part (camel/hump, owl/feathers, etc.) When the cards match, for example, *camel/hump,* the student keeps the cards if she can make a sentence: *Camels have a hump on their back.* When the student can't say the sentence or the cards don't match, the student turns the cards back over.

4. The activity ends when all the cards are gone.

Picture Cards: Pets and Farm Animals

10.4

10.8

10.12

10.16

10.3

10.7

10.11

10.15

10.2

10.6

10.10

10.14

10.1

10.5

10.9

10.13

Word List

10.1 cat
10.2 dog
10.3 rabbit
10.4 mouse
10.5 goldfish
10.6 frog
10.7 turtle
10.8 lizard
10.9 parakeet
10.10 duck
10.11 horse
10.12 sheep
10.13 goat
10.14 pig
10.15 cow
10.16 rooster

Picture Cards: Plants and Animals

10.20	10.24	10.28	10.32
10.19	10.23	10.27	10.31
10.18	10.22	10.26	10.30
10.17	10.21	10.25	10.29

Word List

10.17 palm tree
10.18 pine tree
10.19 rose
10.20 daisy
10.21 squirrel
10.22 chipmunk
10.23 octopus
10.24 eel
10.25 whale
10.26 seal
10.27 penguin
10.28 eagle
10.29 grasshopper
10.30 honeybee
10.31 alligator
10.32 snake

Picture Cards: Mammals

10.36

10.40

10.44

10.48

10.35

10.39

10.43

10.47

10.34

10.38

10.42

10.46

10.33

10.37

10.41

10.45

Word List

10.33 bear
10.34 deer
10.35 dolphin
10.36 elephant
10.37 giraffe
10.38 gorilla
10.39 hippopotamus
10.40 koala
10.41 leopard
10.42 lion
10.43 llama
10.44 monkey
10.45 panda
10.46 tiger
10.47 walrus
10.48 zebra

Picture Cards: Animals/Animal Parts

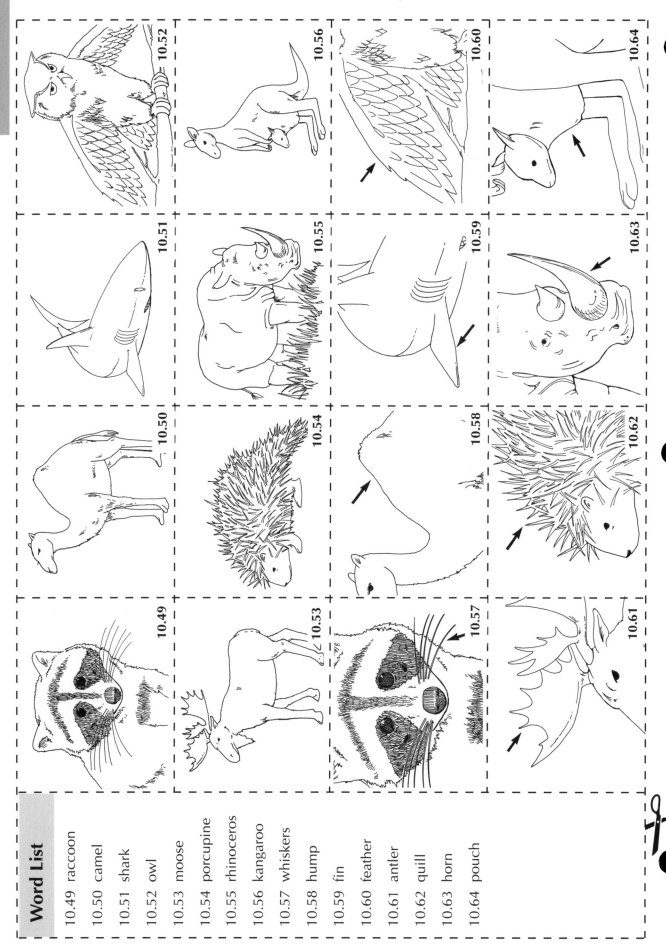

10.52

10.56

10.60

10.64

10.51

10.55

10.59

10.63

10.50

10.54

10.58

10.62

10.49

10.53

10.57

10.61

11. Work

Page(s)	Activity	Jobs and Occupations (136–139)	Job Skills (140)	Job Search (141)	An Office (142–143)	Computers (144)	A Hotel (145)	A Factory (146)	Job Safety (147)	Farming and Ranching (148)	Construction (149)	Tools and Building Supplies (150–151)
166	**This office is a mess!** (Round Table Label)				◆	◆						
167	**What job is best for you?** (Survey)		◆									
168–169	**On the Assembly Line** (Picture Differences)							◆	◆			
170–171	**The Perfect Job for You!** (Information Exchange)	◆	◆	◆								
172	**Four-Star Hotel** (Role Play)						◆					
173	**Work for Yourself or Someone Else?** (Take a Stand)	◆										
174–175	**Work Board Game** (Board Game)	◆	◆	◆	◆	◆	◆	◆	◆	◆	◆	◆
176–180	**Picture Card Activities and Picture Cards**	◆			◆	◆				◆	◆	◆

This office is a mess!

The Oxford Picture Dictionary, pages 142–144. See page xii for Teacher's Notes.

Round Table Label

◆ **Form groups of 4 people.**

◆ **Each person in the group takes turns labeling the items on this paper.**

◆ **After all the pictures have labels, look in the *Dictionary* to check your group's work.**

◆ **What's next?** Test your memory! Your teacher will put 10 office supplies on a desk. Look at them for 15 seconds. Close your eyes while your teacher removes one item. Write down the missing item. Continue playing as the teacher removes more items. Check your "office supply" list with your group.

What job is best for you?

The Oxford Picture Dictionary, page 140. See page xiv for Teacher's Notes.

Survey

- ◆ **Read the survey questions and mark your answers with a ✓.**
- ◆ **Ask and answer the questions again with nine classmates.**
- ◆ **Mark your classmates' answers on the survey form.**

Would you rather...

		My Answers	My Classmates' Answers	No Opinion
...drive a truck or a taxi?	a. truck			
	b. taxi			
...work on a car or a computer?	a. car			
	b. computer			
...sell things in a store or on the phone?	a. store			
	b. phone			
...take care of plants or children?	a. plants			
	b. children			
...use a paintbrush or a hammer?	a. paintbrush			
	b. hammer			
...assist a teacher or a doctor?	a. teacher			
	b. doctor			

- ◆ **Complete the graph below. Chart only student preferences.**

a	b	(Note: Your chart will not show the "No opinion" category.)

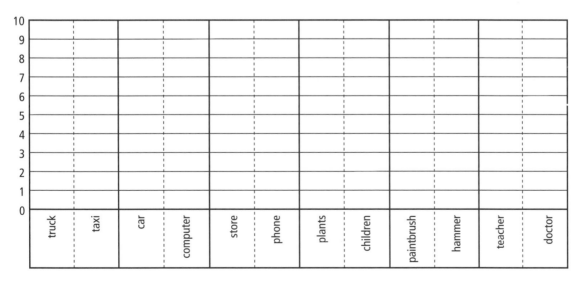

- ◆ **What's next?** Your teacher will ask you for your survey results. Write sentences about the answers. Follow the example below:

  Seven out of ten students would rather drive a truck.

Unit Eleven   167

On the Assembly Line

The Oxford Picture Dictionary, pages 146–147. See page xvi for Teacher's Notes.

Picture Differences

A

- ◆ **Sit with a partner and look at each other's papers.**
- ◆ **There are 10 differences between your pictures.**
- ◆ **Work with your partner to find the differences.**

- ◆ **Write the differences you find on the chart.**

A	B
1. _time clock on wall_	_no time clock on wall_
2.	
3.	
4.	
5.	
6.	
7.	
8.	
9.	
10.	

168 Unit Eleven

© 1999 Oxford University Press   Permission granted to reproduce for classroom use.

On the Assembly Line

The Oxford Picture Dictionary, pages 146–147. See page xvi for Teacher's Notes.

Picture Differences

B

- ◆ Sit with a partner and look at each other's papers.
- ◆ There are 10 differences between your pictures.
- ◆ Work with your partner to find the differences.

- ◆ **Write the differences you find on the chart.**

A	B
1. time clock on wall	no time clock on wall
2.	
3.	
4.	
5.	
6.	
7.	
8.	
9.	
10.	

The Perfect Job for You!

The Oxford Picture Dictionary, pages 136–139, 140–141. See page xviii for Teacher's Notes.

Information Exchange

A

1

- ◆ Sit with a partner. (Don't show this paper to your partner!)
- ◆ Ask your partner about the missing information on the job board below.
- ◆ You can use these questions:

    "What experience do you need?"

    "What are the benefits?"

    "How do you apply?"

- ◆ Write in the missing information and read it back to your partner to check your work.

ABE OCCUPATIONAL CENTER — EMPLOYMENT OPPORTUNITIES

STOCK CLERK
Castillo Lamps

1 year factory exp.
Operate forklift
H.S. graduate pref.

Apply _____

_____
759 Central Ave.

_____

Overtime

DELIVERY PERSON
Pizza Express

_____ /will train
Need own car
Clean driving record

_____
709-8436 ext. 2

Salary + tips
Paid _____

GARDENER
Greenthumbs Nursery

Min. _____
Start immediately
Hard worker

Apply _____
675 Main, Newbridge

_____ job
Good salary, oppty.

CASHIER
China Garden

_____ restaurant exp.
Friendly, avail. weekends

Call _____
Ask for Mr. Li

Flexible hours - eves.,
no weekends

2

- ◆ Use the classified ads below to answer your partner's questions.

Tribune Daily News Employment Opportunities

Help Wanted	Help Wanted	Help Wanted	Help Wanted
DENTAL ASSISTANT **Pediatric Office** Min. 1 yr. exp. Good w/ children Call for interview Dr. Tarica (310) 695-1344 Excel. salary, med/dental Uniform allowance	**AUTO MECHANIC** **Al's Garage** Exp. brakes, tune-up Certified smog tester Apply in person. (No calls.) 5846 Chandler Blvd. Good salary w/bonuses No weekends	**HOUSEKEEPERS** **Restaway Resort** Good references No exp. necessary Call (914) 680-8000 For application & information Permanent job Health & pd. vacation	**SALESPERSONS** **Lacy's Fashions** 3 yrs. retail exp. H.S. graduates only Send for application Attn: Personnel P.O. Box 22, N.Y., N.Y. 10325 Salary + commission 10% store discount

- ◆ **What's next?** Practice a job interview with your partner. Choose one job from this page. Decide who will be the interviewer and applicant. Your teacher will help you make a list of questions. "Why are you interested in this job?" "What are the hours?" Practice asking and answering the questions. Present your interview to the class.

The Perfect Job for You!

The Oxford Picture Dictionary, pages 136–139, 140–141. See page xviii for Teacher's Notes.   Information Exchange

 1

◆ Sit with a partner. (Don't show this paper to your partner!)

◆ Use the job board below to answer your partner's questions.

ABE OCCUPATIONAL CENTER — EMPLOYMENT OPPORTUNITIES

STOCK CLERK	DELIVERY PERSON	GARDENER	CASHIER
Castillo Lamps	**Pizza Express**	**Greenthumbs Nursery**	**China Garden**
1 year factory exp.	No exp. nec/will train	Min. 1 yr. exp.	Good math skills
Operate forklift	Need own car	Start immediately	1 yr. restaurant exp.
H.S. graduate pref.	Clean driving record	Hard worker	Friendly, avail. weekends
Apply in person	Call for application	Apply Tues./Thurs.,	Call 769-2561
3PM – 11 PM	709-8436 ext. 2	675 Main, Newbridge	Ask for Mr. Li
759 Central Ave.	Salary + tips	Year-round job	Flexible hours - eves.,
2 wks. vacation	Paid mileage	Good salary, oppty.	no weekends
Overtime			

 2

◆ Ask your partner about the missing information in the classifed ads below.

◆ You can use these questions:

   "What experience do you need?"

   "What are the benefits?"

   "How do you apply?"

◆ Write in the missing information and read it back to your partner to check your work.

Tribune Daily News Employment Opportunities

Help Wanted	Help Wanted	Help Wanted	Help Wanted
DENTAL ASSISTANT Pediatric Office	**AUTO MECHANIC** Al's Garage	**HOUSEKEEPERS** Restaway Resort	**SALESPERSONS** Lacy's Fashions
Min. 1 yr. exp.	_____, tune-up	Good references	_____exp.
Good w/ children	Certified smog tester	No exp. _____	H.S. graduates only
_____	Apply_____.(No calls.)	Call (914) 680-8000	_____application
Dr. Tarica_____	5846 Chandler Blvd.	For_____& information	Attn: Personnel
Excel. salary,_____	Good salary w/bonuses	_____job	P.O. Box 22, N.Y., N.Y. 10325
Uniform allowance	No weekends	_____& pd. vacation	Salary + commission
			_____store discount

◆ **What's next?** Practice a job interview with your partner. Choose one job from this page. Decide who will be the interviewer and applicant. Your teacher will help you make a list of questions. "Why are you interested in this job?" "What are the hours?" Practice asking and answering the questions. Present your interview to the class.

Four-Star Hotel

The Oxford Picture Dictionary, page 145. See page xix for Teacher's Notes.

- ◆ **Form groups of 4 people.**
- ◆ **Practice saying all the lines.**
- ◆ **Choose your character and decide what you will say.**
- ◆ **Think of other things your character can say.**
- ◆ **Act out your role play.**

THE CHARACTERS:
a happy guest
an unhappy guest
a desk clerk
a bell captain

THE SCENE:
A hotel. Hotel workers are helping several guests.

THE PROPS:
a bell
a key
a small suitcase
a handwritten hotel "bill"

THE SCRIPT:

Who says...	...these lines?
an unhappy guest	Can I change rooms? The <u>heater</u>* doesn't work.
	We don't <u>change reservations</u>. The <u>front desk</u> can help you.
	This place is <u>great</u>! It has <u>three pools</u>!
	Is it possible to stay <u>one more night</u>?
	Yes, we can change your check-out time. How about <u>1 p.m.</u>?
	Meet you at the <u>gift shop</u>. I need to buy some postcards.
	Your total for room service is <u>$25.50</u>.
	What? I didn't order <u>dinner</u> in my room!
	I lost a <u>brown bag</u>. Can you check the luggage cart?
	I'll call the bell hop. He'll be here in <u>two</u> minutes.
	Here's a key for guest room <u>#225</u>. It's down the hall <u>on the right</u>.

* You can substitute other vocabulary for the underlined words.

- ◆ **What's next?** Pretend you are opening a new hotel in your city. Get paper and markers from your teacher. Work with your group to design a hotel for both families and business travelers. Draw your ideas and share them with the class.

Work for Yourself or Someone Else?

The Oxford Picture Dictionary, pages 136–139. See page xx for Teacher's Notes.

Take a Stand

- ◆ **Think about the reasons to work for yourself or work for someone else.**
- ◆ **Read each statement on the list.**
- ◆ **If the statement shows that <u>working for yourself</u> is a good idea, make a ✓ in that column.**
- ◆ **If the statement shows that <u>working for someone else</u> is a good idea, make a ✓ in that column.**
- ◆ **For K and L, think of two more statements to add to this list.**

STATEMENTS	working for yourself	working for someone else
A. Many employers pay for their workers' health insurance.		
B. Some companies give two weeks paid vacation.		
C. The goverment gives loans to people starting small businesses.		
D. You can work with your family in your own business.		
E. Nobody can fire you if you are the boss.		
F. More experienced workers can help you learn on the job.		
G. You have more job security if you work for someone else.		
H. Some jobs pay for cars, uniforms and travel expenses.		
I. In your own business, you make your own work schedule.		
J. You can do the kind of work you like in your own business.		
K.		
L.		

- ◆ **Sit with a partner and compare papers.**
- ◆ **Write your and your partner's ideas.**

    I think working for _____ *is a good/bad idea because* _____

    _____.

    My partner thinks working for _____ is a good/bad idea

    because _____.

- ◆ **What's next?** Take a stand. Your teacher will tell you where to stand if you support working for yourself and where to stand if you support working for someone else.

Work Board

 tape here

Draw
something
you see in a
hotel.
Describe it.

In 15
seconds...
name 5 jobs
where people
make things.

Pick a
tools card.
Say 3 things
about it.

Answer:
What job skill would
you like to
learn? Why?

In 15
seconds...
name 5 things at
a construction area.

Act out
a job for your group.
(The group has to
guess what it is!)

To begin...

- Put your markers on start.
- Take turns flipping a coin to move your marker around the board.

moves
one
space

moves
two
spaces

- Follow the directions on the squares.
- Ask your group for help when you don't know the answer.

Finish

Pick
a tools card.

Spell it.

Start

Name 5 things that can grow on a farm.

 tape here

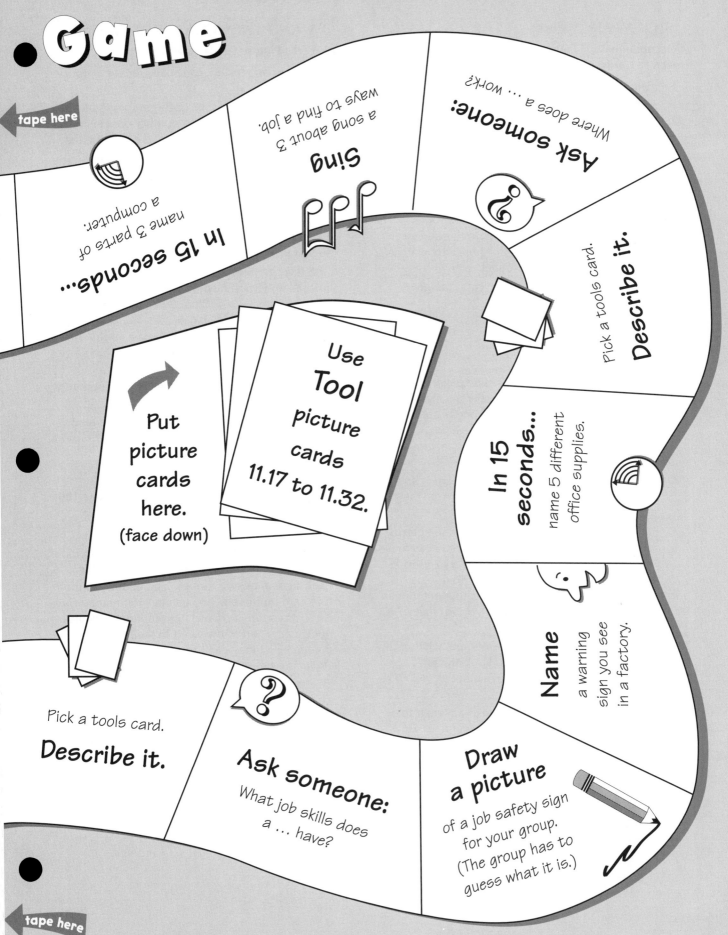

Game

tape here

In 15 seconds...
name 3 parts of
a computer.

Sing
a song about 3
ways to find a job.

Ask someone:
Where does a ... work?

Pick a tools card.
Describe it.

Put
picture
cards
here.
(face down)

Use
Tool
picture
cards
11.17 to 11.32.

In 15
seconds...
name 5 different
office supplies.

Name
a warning
sign you see
in a factory.

Pick a tools card.
Describe it.

Ask someone:
What job skills does
a ... have?

Draw
a picture
of a job safety sign
for your group.
(The group has to
guess what it is.)

tape here

Work Picture Card Activities

PICK A PAIR (Pairs)

Occupations and Equipment/Supplies Picture Cards, page 177

1. Pair students and give each pair one picture card page.

2. Have the pair cut up the cards, shuffle them and place them face down in four rows of four cards.

3. Have partners take turns turning over two cards at a time, trying to match related occupations and equipment/supplies. When the cards match, for example, *secretary/typewriter* the student keeps the cards if she can say a sentence: *A secretary uses a typewriter.* When the student can't say the sentence or the cards don't match, the student turns the cards back over.

4. The activity ends when all the cards are gone.

TWIN GRIDS (Pairs)

**Tools Picture Cards, page 178
Grid, page 197**

1. Duplicate one copy of the grid on page 197. Write in 16 numbers, one number per square. Give each student one grid and one picture card page. (If you have an overhead projector, see Using the Overhead Projector in the Picture Cards Teacher's Notes, page x.)

2. Have students cut apart their picture cards and place them face up, on their desks next to the grid.

3. Tell students that each numbered box represents an aisle in a hardware store. Direct students to find the picture of the hammer, and place this picture on the grid square with #1 in it. Encourage students to ask clarification questions. *Did you say hammer or handsaw? Was that #1 or #11?*

4. Continue telling students where to put what until all the grid squares are filled. Have students compare their grids with one another as you clarify any discrepancies.

5. Next pair students. Give each pair a manila folder to use as a screen between the partners. Have one partner (the sender) tell the other (the receiver) *Put the hammer in aisle #1.* [Students do not have to copy your sentences.] Both partners place their pictures on the grids. When the grids are complete, senders and receivers compare their grids.

6. Have senders and receivers switch roles.

NOW AND THEN CHARADES (Groups)

Work Verbs Picture Cards, page 179

1. Duplicate one picture card page for each group of 4-5 students.

2. Group students and give each group one picture card page. Tell students to number off. Have #1 cut apart the picture cards. Have #2 shuffle the cards and place them face down on a desk. Identify #4 as the recorder.

3. For the first round, Student #1 picks a card from the deck, asks *What am I doing?* and pantomimes the action until the group can name it. Once the group names the action: You're painting a fence. Student #1 sits down.

4. The recorder then asks the group: *What did Carlos do?* Group members reach consensus on the correct way to put the sentence in the past, using the **Verb Guide** pages 170–172 in the *Dictionary* to check the correct past tense form. The recorder writes the groups' response on a sheet of paper. *Carlos painted a fence.*

5. Student #2 picks a card and the activity continues.

6. The activity is over when all the students in the group have had two turns. Recorders can read from or turn in their papers.

GUESS WHAT? (Groups)

Work Places/Work Supplies Picture Cards, page 180

1. Have students form small groups of 2-4 students.

2. Give each group one page of cut-up picture cards. Have one student in the group shuffle the cards and place them face down on the table.

3. Each student takes a turn picking up the top picture card on the pile and giving a definition. *This protects your head.* (hard hat) Caution students to <u>not</u> use any part of the word in their definition. For example, they can't say, *This is a hat that protects your head.*

4. The other group members try to guess the word. The first student to guess the word keeps the picture card.

5. The activity ends when all the cards are guessed correctly.

Picture Cards: Occupations and Equipment/Supplies

11.4

11.8

11.12

11.16

11.3

11.7

11.11

11.15

11.2

11.6

11.10

11.14

11.1

11.5

11.9

11.13

Word List

11.1 secretary

11.2 farmworker

11.3 construction worker

11.4 computer programmer

11.5 accountant

11.6 welder

11.7 garment worker

11.8 packer

11.9 typewriter

11.10 tractor

11.11 crane

11.12 computer

11.13 calculator

11.14 safety goggles

11.15 sewing machine

11.16 packing tape

Picture Cards: Tools

Picture Cards: Work Verbs

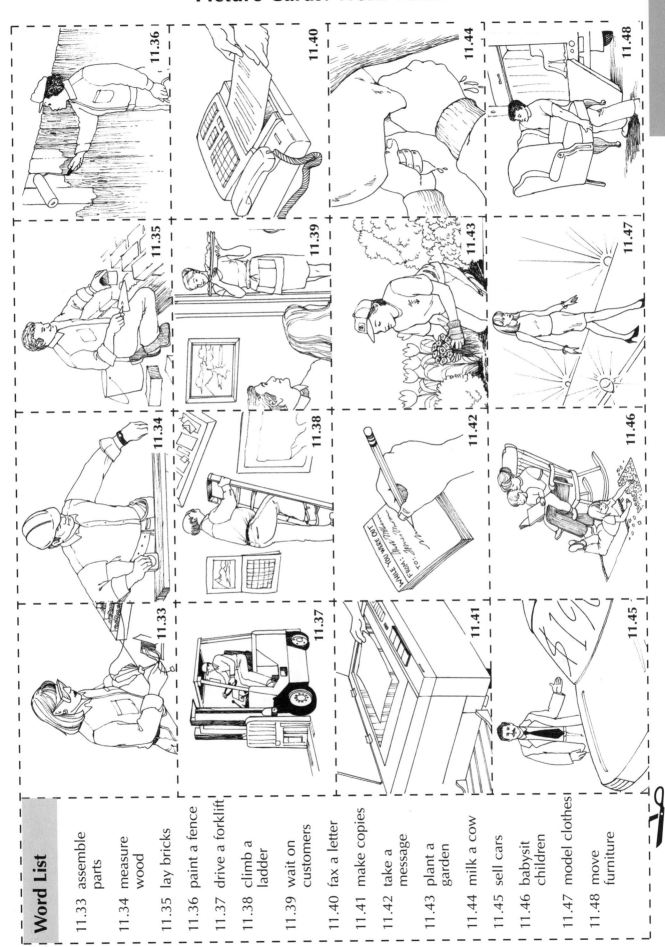

Word List

11.33 assemble parts
11.34 measure wood
11.35 lay bricks
11.36 paint a fence
11.37 drive a forklift
11.38 climb a ladder
11.39 wait on customers
11.40 fax a letter
11.41 make copies
11.42 take a message
11.43 plant a garden
11.44 milk a cow
11.45 sell cars
11.46 babysit children
11.47 model clothes
11.48 move furniture

Picture Cards: Work Places/Work Supplies

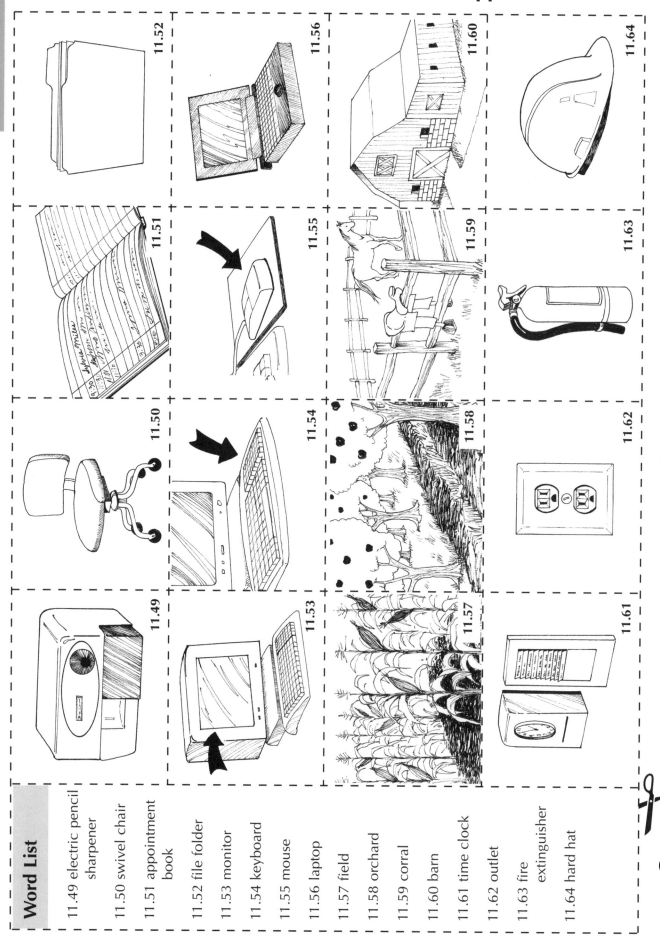

11.52 · 11.56 · 11.60 · 11.64
11.51 · 11.55 · 11.59 · 11.63
11.50 · 11.54 · 11.58 · 11.62
11.49 · 11.53 · 11.57 · 11.61

Word List

11.49 electric pencil sharpener
11.50 swivel chair
11.51 appointment book
11.52 file folder
11.53 monitor
11.54 keyboard
11.55 mouse
11.56 laptop
11.57 field
11.58 orchard
11.59 corral
11.60 barn
11.61 time clock
11.62 outlet
11.63 fire extinguisher
11.64 hard hat

12. Recreation

Page(s)		Places to Go (152)	The Park and Playground (153)	Outdoor Recreation (154)	The Beach (155)	Sports Verbs (156–157)	Team Sports (158)	Individual Sports (159)	Winter Sports and Water Sports (160)	Sports Equipment (161)	Hobbies and Games (162–163)	Electronics and Photography (164–165)	Entertainment (166–167)	Holidays (168)	A Party (169)
182	**A Camping Trip!** (Round Table Label)			◆											
183	**Checkers, anyone?** (Mixer)										◆				
184–185	**Coming Up in Los Angeles!** (Information Exchange)	◆													
186–187	**Holidays and a Party** (Double Crossword)													◆	◆
188	**So Many Programs— So Many Choices!** (Role Play)												◆		
189	**Learn About Religious Holidays in School— Yes or No?** (Take a Stand)														◆
190–191	**Recreation Board Game** (Board Game)	◆	◆	◆	◆	◆	◆	◆	◆	◆	◆	◆	◆	◆	◆
192–196	**Picture Card Activities and Picture Cards**	◆				◆	◆	◆				◆			

A Camping Trip!

The Oxford Picture Dictionary, page 154. See page xii for Teacher's Notes.

- ◆ **Form groups of 4 people.**
- ◆ **Each person in the group takes turns labeling the items on this paper.**
- ◆ **After all the pictures have labels, look in the *Dictionary* to check your group's work.**

matches

- ◆ **What's next?** Pretend you are going on a camping trip but can only take three items. Take turns telling your group which three items you would choose and why.

© 1999 Oxford University Press   Permission granted to reproduce for classroom use.

Checkers, anyone?

●

◆ **Write the missing letters for each word.**

◆ **Walk around the room. Ask and answer the questions.**

◆ **Write a different name in each box.**

Do you play checkers?

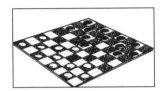

1. Do you play _c h e c k e r s_ ?

Yes	No

2. Do you play _v _ _ _ _ _   g _ _ _ _ _ _ ?

Yes	No

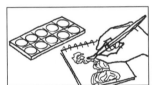

3. Do you _p _ _ _ _ _ ?

Yes	No

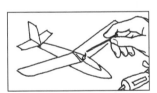

4. Do you _b _ _ _ _ _ _   m _ _ _ _ _ _ _ ?

Yes	No

5. Do you have a _s _ _ _ _ _ _   c _ _ _ _ _ _ _ _ _ _ ?

Yes	No

6. Do you _k _ _ _ _ ?

Yes	No

7. Do you _p _ _ _ _   c _ _ _ _ _ ?

Yes	No

◆ **What's next?** Discuss your answers with your class.

Coming Up in Los Angeles!

The Oxford Picture Dictionary, page 152. See page xviii for Teacher's Notes.

A

- ◆ Sit with a partner. (Don't show this paper to your partner!)
- ◆ Ask your partner about the missing information in the calendar section of the newspaper below.
- ◆ You can use these questions:

    What is happening at _____? What hours is it open?

    How much does it cost for a _____ to go there?

    How much is parking at the _____?

- ◆ Write in the missing information and read it back to your partner to check your work.

- ◆ **What's next?** Work with a partner. Make a list of those places you would like to go if you visit Los Angeles. List only those places both you and your partner agree on.

Coming Up in Los Angeles!

The Oxford Picture Dictionary, page 152. See page xviii for Teacher's Notes.

◆ **Sit with a partner. (Don't show this paper to your partner!)**

◆ **Ask your partner about the missing information in the calendar section of the newspaper below.**

◆ **You can use these questions:**

What is happening at ———————? *What hours is it open?*

How much does it cost for a ——————— *to go there?*

How much is parking at the ———————?

◆ **Write in the missing information and read it back to your partner to check your work.**

CALENDAR OF EVENTS

LOS ANGELES COUNTY ART MUSEUM

Picasso – His Early Work

Sept. 30 – Oct. 21st

HOURS
Tues.–Thurs. 10 am – 5 pm
Fri. 10 am – 9 pm
Sat., Sun. 11 am – 6 pm

ADMISSION
Adults $6.00   Seniors $4.00
Students $4.00
Parking: $5.00

VALLEY INDOOR SWAPMEET

Over 400 Booths! Halloween Costumes Too!

This weekend, October_____

Fri., Sat., Sun. ____ – ____
Admission $ ____
Children and Seniors: ____
Parking: ____

LOS ANGELES ZOO

See Oho the Baby Panda!!

Arriving Sept. 28th!
Daily 10 am – 5 pm

Admission:
Adults: $8.25
Children: $3.25
Seniors: $5.25
Parking: Free

DODGER STADIUM

DODGERS VS. GIANTS

OCT._____

Game time:_____
General Admission: $____
Parking: $____

The Huntington Library Botanical Gardens

Roses! Roses! Roses!

October 15–25
Tues. – Sun.
10:30 am – 4:30 pm

Admission:
Adults: $7.50   Students: $4.00
Seniors: $6.00   Parking: Free

LOS ANGELES COUNTY FAIR

World's Largest County Fair!

Sept.____ – ____

Mon. – Thur. ____ – ____
Fri. ____ – ____   Sat. ____ – ____
Sun. ____ – ____

General Admission: $____
Seniors: $____
Children: $____
Parking: $____

MATINEE TODAY!
Sherman Oaks Movie Theater
SPY MY SPY
Sun. – Thur. 1:00, 4:00, 7:00, 10:00

Adults: $7.50
Children: $3.50
Seniors: $4.50
Matinee: $4.00
Parking: Free

HALLOWEEN CARNIVAL

SUN RIDGE PARK
OCTOBER ____
____ – ____
Admission: $____
Parking:____

◆ **What's next?** Work with a partner. Make a list of those places you would like to go if you visit Los Angeles. List only those places both you and your partner agree on.

Holidays and a Party

The Oxford Picture Dictionary, pages 168–169. See page xvii for Teacher's Notes.

Double Crossword

A

♦ **Sit with a partner. (Don't show this paper to your partner!)**

♦ **Take turns giving the clues to complete the puzzle.**

   1 across — This holiday is on the first day of the year

♦ **If your partner needs help, give one letter from the answer on your puzzle.**

   The second letter is E.

♦ **When both puzzles are complete, compare your work.**

Clues

1 across — This holiday is on the first day of the year

4 across — A holiday in November when people give thanks

5 across — Children wear costumes on this holiday

7 across — A holiday on December 25th

11 across — The holiday when people watch fireworks

12 across — This shape means, "I love you."

14 across — Many cities have one of these on July 4th

16 across — A holiday in February about love

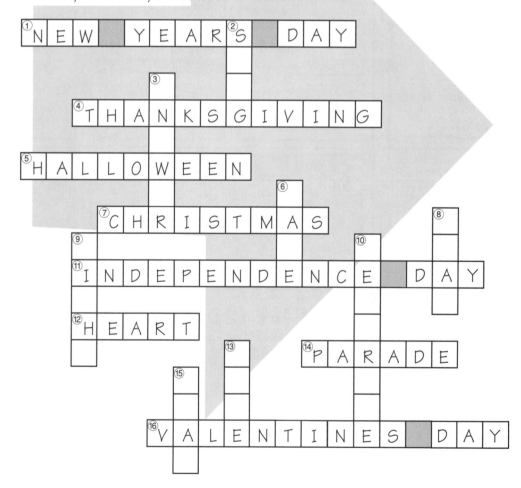

© 1999 Oxford University Press   Permission granted to reproduce for classroom use.

Holidays and a Party

The Oxford Picture Dictionary, pages 168–169. See page xvii for Teacher's Notes.

Double Crossword

B

- ◆ **Sit with a partner. (Don't show this paper to your partner!)**
- ◆ **Take turns giving the clues to complete the puzzle.**

  2 down — To use your voice to make music

- ◆ **If your partner needs help, give one letter from the answer on your puzzle.**

  The second letter is L.

- ◆ **When both puzzles are complete, compare your work.**

Clues

2 down — To use your voice to make music

3 down — What you do when the doorbell rings

6 down — People... a wish when they blow out the candles.

8 down — To think about everything you need to do for the party

9 down — What you do to candles to make them burn

10 down — What you do to the house to make it pretty

13 down — What people do at the beginning of a surprise party

15 down — What people do to a present before they give it

So Many Programs—So Many Choices!

Role Play

- ◆ Form groups of 4 people.
- ◆ Practice saying all the lines.
- ◆ Choose your character and decide what you will say.
- ◆ Think of other things your character can say.
- ◆ Act out your role play.

THE PROPS:
the TV listings from a newspaper
some chairs

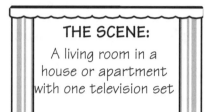

THE SCENE:
A living room in a house or apartment with one television set

THE CHARACTERS:
a senior
a middle-aged person
a teenager
a child
(living in the same apartment)

THE SCRIPT:

Who says...	...these lines?
a senior	O.K., everyone, what do you want to watch tonight?
	Is there a good movie* on?
	Let's watch a soap opera, all the movies are old.
	I love a good science fiction story.
	Please, nothing with monsters. I get nightmares!
	A western, let's watch a western!
	We always watch westerns. Can't we watch something else?
	Romance is my favorite.
	Not a romance, please. They're boring.
	I really don't like anything but game shows.
	Nature programs are interesting.
	Let's watch this new comedy, *Love Me Tonight*!
	Can't we watch a cartoon? I never get to watch cartoons!

* You can substitute other vocabulary for the underlined words.

- ◆ **What's next?** Tell what happens when people in your home want to watch different programs on television.

Learn About Religious Holidays in School—Yes or No?

The Oxford Picture Dictionary, page 168. See page xx for Teacher's Notes.

Take a Stand

- ◆ **Think about the reasons to learn about religious holidays in school.**
- ◆ **Read each statement on the list.**
- ◆ **If the statement shows that learning about religious holidays in school is <u>a good idea</u>, make a ✓ in that column.**
- ◆ **If the statement shows that learning about religious holidays in school is <u>not a good idea</u>, make a ✓ in that column.**
- ◆ **For K and L, think of two more statements to add to this list.**

STATEMENTS	+	–
A. Religious holidays can be fun.		
B. Religious holidays have special foods.		
C. People learn about each other by learning about their holidays.		
D. In the United States, church and government are separate.		
E. There is not enough time to learn academic subjects like reading and math.		
F. Students are absent sometimes because of religious holidays.		
G. Religious holidays are serious for some people.		
H. Everyone celebrates religious holidays differently.		
I. Some parents do not want their children learning about other religions at school.		
J. Religion can be an important part of life.		
K.		
L.		

- ◆ **Sit with a partner and compare papers.**
- ◆ **Write your and your partner's ideas.**

I think it is _____ to learn about religious holidays in school because

_____ .

My partner thinks it is _____ to learn about religious holidays in school

because _____ .

- ◆ **What's next?** Write four sentences on how you celebrate a special holiday.

Recreation Board.

tape here →

Draw something you see at a park.

Name one winter sport.

Pick a recreation card. Say 3 things about it.

Answer: What kinds of TV programs do you watch?

In 15 seconds... name 5 kinds of sports equipment.

Act out a water sport for your group. (The group has to guess what it is!)

To begin...

- Put your markers on start.
- Take turns flipping a coin to move your marker around the board.

moves one space

moves two spaces

- Follow the directions on the squares.
- Ask your group for help when you don't know the answer.

Finish

Start

Pick a recreation card. **Spell it.**

Name something you use at the beach.

tape here →

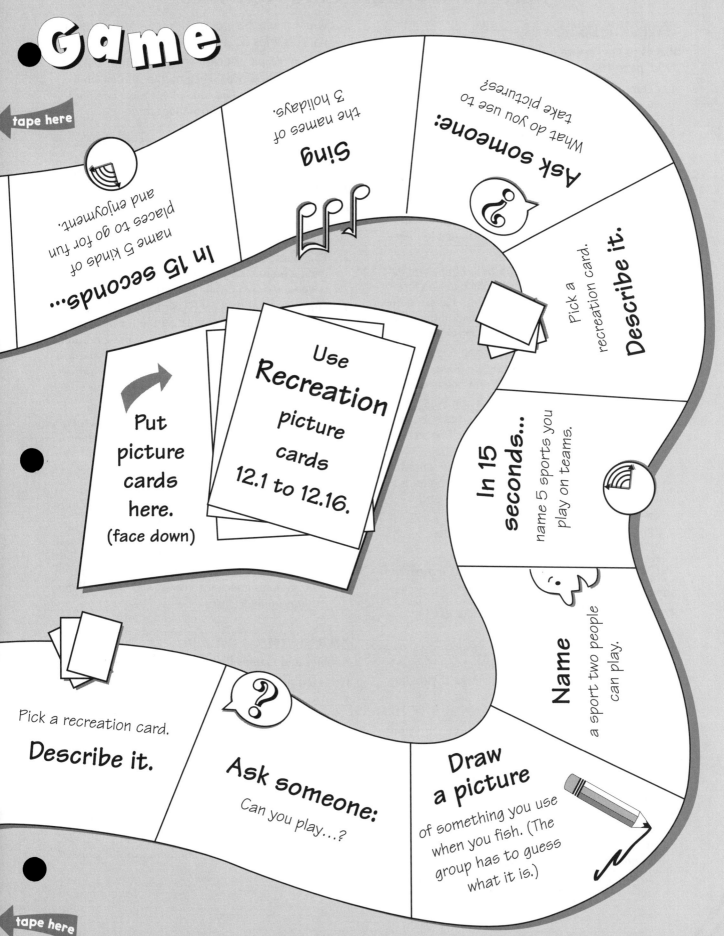

Game

Recreation Picture Card Activities

TWIN GRIDS (Pairs)

Places to Go Picture Cards, page 193
Grid, page 197

1. Duplicate one copy of the grid, page 197 and write in the names of students in the class, one name per square. (You can put in other names if you don't want use the names of your students.) Give each student one grid and one picture card page. (If you have an overhead projector, see Using the Overhead Projector in the Picture Cards Teacher's Notes, page x.)

2. Have students cut apart their picture cards and place them face up on their desks next to their grid.

3. Tell students, *Elena went to the art museum last weekend.* Direct students to place the picture of the art museum on the square with Elena's name. Encourage students to ask clarification questions. *Who went? Did you say the art museum?*

4. Continue telling students where all the students went until all the grid squares are filled. Have students compare their grids with one another.

5. Pair students and give each pair a manila folder to use as a screen between the partners. Have one partner (the sender) tell the other (the receiver). _____ *went to the* _____. (Students do not have to copy your sentences.) Both partners place their pictures on the grids. When the grids are complete, senders and receivers compare their grids.

6. Have senders and receivers switch roles.

NOW AND THEN CHARADES (Groups)

Sports Verbs Picture Cards, page 194

1. Duplicate one picture card page for each group of 4-5 students.

2. Group students and give each group one picture card page. Tell students to number off. Have #1 cut apart the picture cards. Have #2 shuffle the cards and place them face down on a desk. Identify #4 as the recorder.

3. For the first round, Student #1 picks a card from the deck and pantomimes the action, asking, *What am I doing?* She continues pantomiming until a student from the group can name the action. *You are kicking a ball.*

4. The recorder then asks the group, What did Carlos do? Group members reach consensus on the correct way to write the sentence. (They may use the **Verb Guide** on pages 170–172 in the *Dictionary* to check the spelling.) The recorder

writes down the group's response on a sheet of paper. *Carlos kicked the ball.*

5. Student #2 picks a card and the activity continues.

6. The activity is over when all the students in the group have had two turns. Recorders can read from their papers or turn them in.

PEER DICTATION (Pairs)

Team Sports and Individual Sports Picture Cards, page 195

1. Duplicate a class set of the picture card pages and cut off the Word List on the sidebar. (Hold on to these for step 6.)

2. Pair students and give Student A and Student B each a picture card page. Have Student A put her page face down until it is her turn.

3. Direct Student B in each pair to look at page 158 in the *Dictionary* and read off the list of Team Sports. When Student A hears a Team Sport that is on her picture page, she *says I have that. How do you spell it?* Student B spells out the word so that Student A can write it under the picture.

4. When Student A has written all of the team sports, she puts her paper aside. Student B then gets a picture card page and listens to Student A read the list of Individual Sports from page 159 in the *Dictionary*. Student B writes the names of the individual sports under those pictures.

5. Both students then write the words for the pictures not yet labelled (Student A writes down the Individual Sports, Student B writes down the Team Sports). They then compare their answers.

6. Distribute the class set of the cut Word List and have students check the correct spelling of all the pictures on their pages.

GUESS WHAT? (Groups)

Hobbies and Games Picture Cards, page 196

1. Have students form small groups of 2-4 students.

2. Give each group one page of cut-up picture cards. Have one student in the group shuffle the cards and place them face down on the table.

3. Each student takes a turn picking up the top picture card on the pile and giving a definition. *You use this to take a picture. It uses film.*

4. The other group members try to guess the word. The first student to guess the word keeps the picture card.

5. The activity ends when all the cards are guessed correctly.

Picture Cards: Places to Go

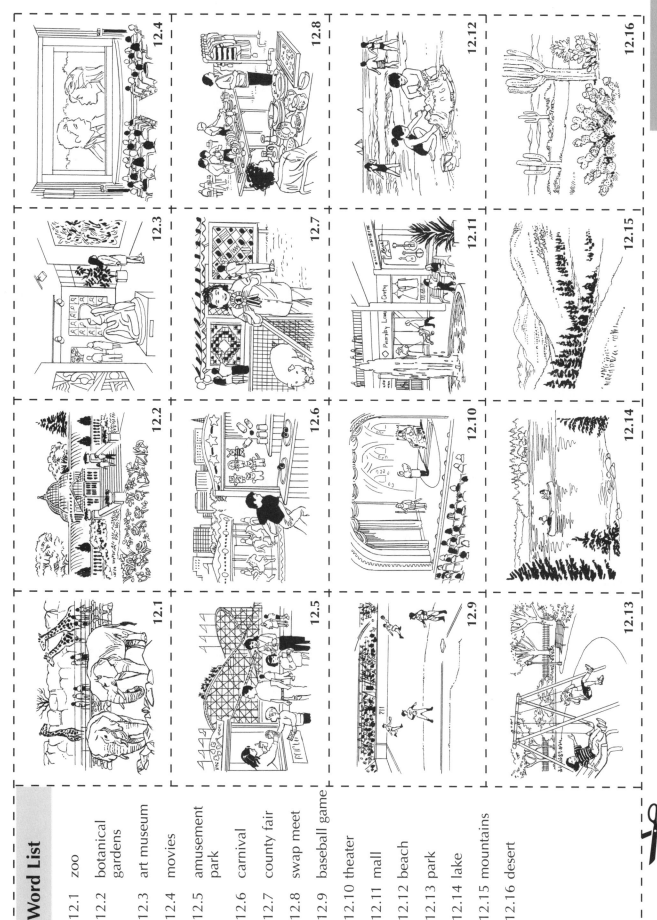

Picture Cards: Sports Verbs

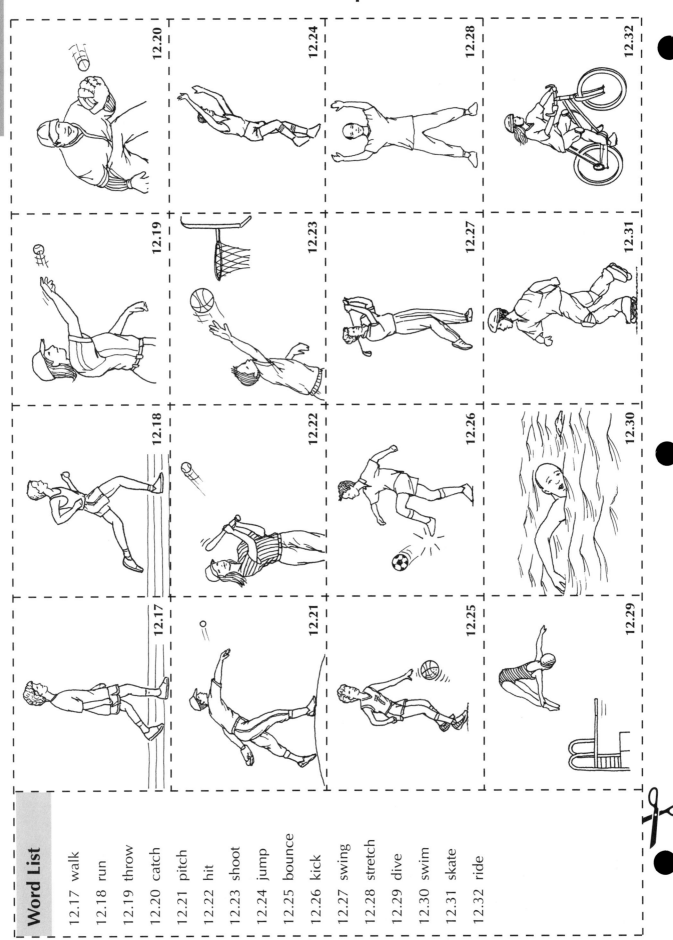

12.20

12.24

12.28

12.32

12.19

12.23

12.27

12.31

12.18

12.22

12.26

12.30

12.17

12.21

12.25

12.29

Word List
12.17 walk
12.18 run
12.19 throw
12.20 catch
12.21 pitch
12.22 hit
12.23 shoot
12.24 jump
12.25 bounce
12.26 kick
12.27 swing
12.28 stretch
12.29 dive
12.30 swim
12.31 skate
12.32 ride

194 Unit Twelve

Picture Cards: Team Sports and Individual Sports

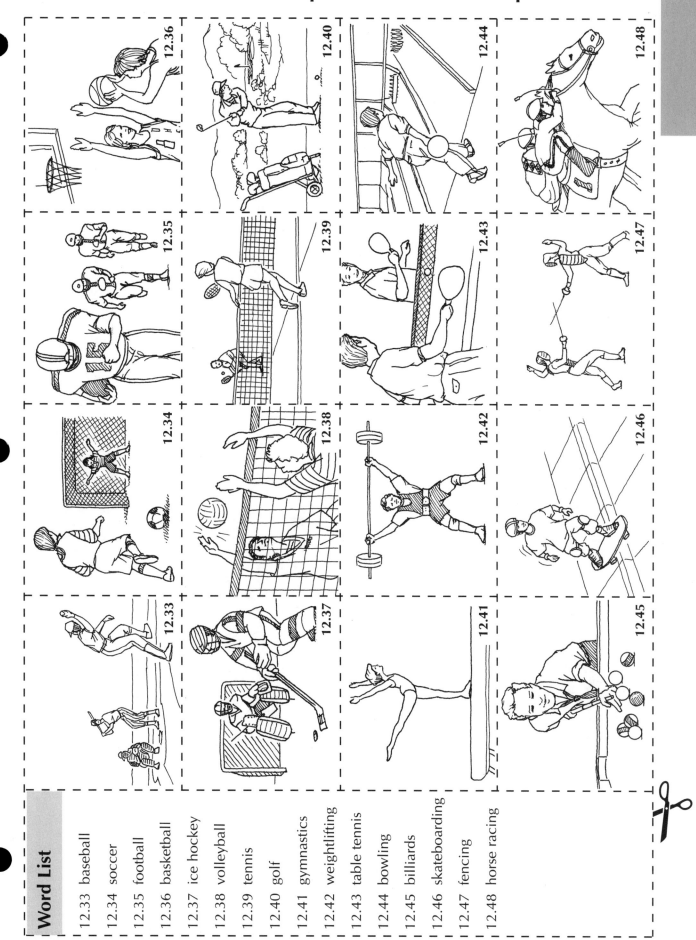

12.36 · 12.40 · 12.44 · 12.48
12.35 · 12.39 · 12.43 · 12.47
12.34 · 12.38 · 12.42 · 12.46
12.33 · 12.37 · 12.41 · 12.45

Word List

12.33 baseball
12.34 soccer
12.35 football
12.36 basketball
12.37 ice hockey
12.38 volleyball
12.39 tennis
12.40 golf
12.41 gymnastics
12.42 weightlifting
12.43 table tennis
12.44 bowling
12.45 billiards
12.46 skateboarding
12.47 fencing
12.48 horse racing

Picture Cards: Hobbies and Games

12.52

12.56

12.60

12.64

12.51

12.55

12.59

12.63

12.50

12.54

12.58

12.62

12.49

12.53

12.57

12.61

Blank Grid

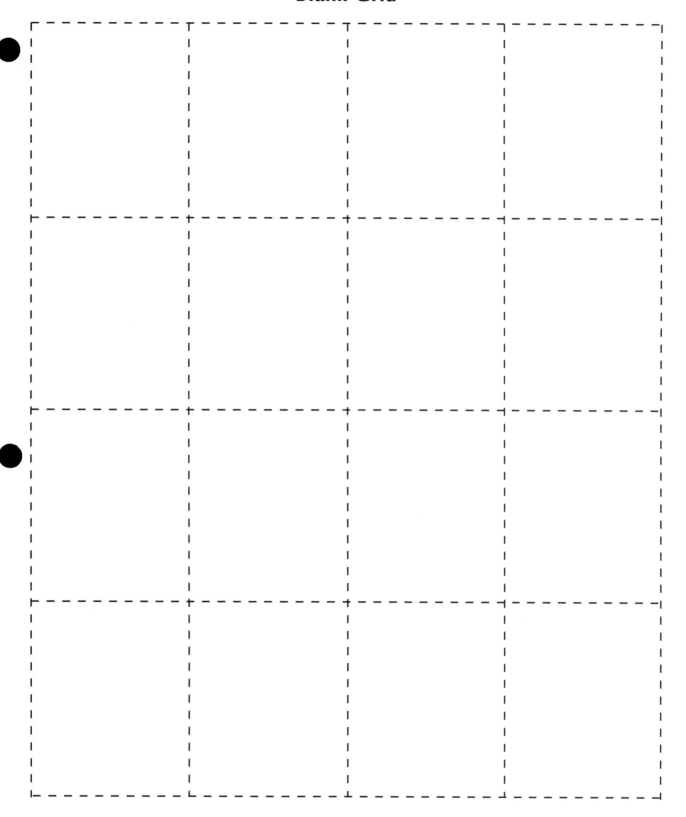

197

Activity Index

Take a Stand

Board Game

Picture Card Activities

A–Z

PICK A PAIR

TWIN GRIDS